D0855601

Flood Stage and Rising

Flood Stage and Rising

Jane Varley

UNIVERSITY OF NEBRASKA PRESS
LINCOLN AND LONDON

Excerpts from "Ask Me," copyright
1977, 1998, by the Estate of William
Stafford, are reprinted from *The Way
It Is: New and Selected Poems* with the
permission of Graywolf Press,
Saint Paul, Minnesota.

A portion of the poem "Traveling
through Idaho on Opening Day" by
Jim Heynen from *Idaho's Poetry: A
Centennial Anthology*, edited by Ron-
ald E. McFarland and William Stude-
baker, Moscow: University of Idaho
Press, 1988, is used with permission
of the author.

Set in Quadraat and Quadraat Sans
by Kim Essman. Designed by R. W.
Boeche. Printed by Thomson-Shore, Inc.

Library of Congress
Cataloging-in-Publication Data
Varley, Jane.
Flood stage and rising / Jane Varley.
p. cm. ISBN 0-8032-4678-1
(hardcover : alk. paper)
1. Grand Forks (N.D.)—History—20th
century.   2. Floods—North Dakota—
Grand Forks—History—20th century.
3. Fires—North Dakota—Grand Forks
—History—20th century.   4. Varley,
Jane.   5. Grand Forks (N.D.)—Biog-
raphy.   6. Natural history—North
Dakota —Grand Forks.   I. Title.
F644.G8V37 2005
978.4′16033—dc22
2004017237

To the people of Grand Forks

Contents

Acknowledgments

This book, from its very first draft, has felt like a collaborative experience with the communities of the Red River valley in North Dakota and Minnesota. I am grateful to have learned about the passionate, determined, and hardy spirit of those places. Also, I am thankful for the friends who navigated the floodwaters with me, Melanie Crow, Jennifer Bottinelli, Brian White, Steve Almquist, Simon Buehrer, and Stephen Dilks, and the professors who taught me about hearing poetry and seeing nature, Jay Meek and Jim McKenzie. I owe a special debt to the *Grand Forks Herald* for its incredible coverage of the flood; I admire the staff's almost unbelievable feat, never missing a day's news even as their offices burned down.

My writing process is supported, year in and year out, by my ever-amazing and inspiring Free Range writers group—Kim, Buddy, Lisa, and Collin, you give me insight, confidence, and joy in my life and writing.

Friends at Muskingum College have supported my process, and I'd like especially to thank Polly Farquhar, Meghan Fox, Vivian Wagner, Donna Edsall, and Rhoda Van Tassel for reading and commenting on portions of this project.

Also, I am grateful to Ladette Randolph for her faith in my story and to the superb editing and publishing team at the University of Nebraska Press.

I want to thank my family members for their crucial support. My parents, Bob and Barb, are not only great parents but also interesting people who inspire me to think about communities and landscapes. I admire and learn from my sister Chris's resilience through multifaceted challenges. In a very direct sense, I learn from my brother Doug, an English teacher and coach, who read my manuscript with an eagle eye and has been a good friend to me from my earliest memories. My brother Charlie has been there for me through sun dogs, sea discoveries, and traveling on the solstice; we have been miles and miles together. To my extended family, too, I offer thanks: my aunts, Kay O'Brien and Clarice Flagel, and parents-in-law, Wanda and Earl Atkins.

Finally, I want to thank my immediate family, Sam for his companionship, Iris for changing my focus, and last and most, thank you to Gary Atkins, my love and my partner, for helping me understand the floods of the past and making me look forward to finding new waters.

Flood Stage and Rising

One The Red River of the North

North Dakota. I liked the sound of it, the idea of it, the promise of its white space as it appeared in the atlas, an inviting blankness between highways and towns, but cold rain poured down, curtaining the state border as my husband, Gary, and I arrived. The farther north we went, the more dark and rainy it got. Wintry, even. It was May.

We left I-94, our route through Minnesota, and started due north on I-29 into northern North Dakota. With so little traffic, we focused on the freeway pavement, the straightness emphasized by the stark landscape and ice heaves cracking the edges. Billboards seemed enormous in the flat, blank terrain: a seed company, a duty-free store at the Canadian border, the mall at Grand Forks. Massive fields with chunky, black soil filled spaces between farms, and long stretches of stark, battered trees, bowed from the western wind, marked the borders. When we pulled off at a gas station, we parked next to two horses tethered at the gas pumps. Our eyes met. What sort of place was this?

Gary studied the trees along the freeway as we set out again. "They're not even budding yet." He was used to the lush greens and blossoms at this time of year in his home state, Virginia, which we were leaving for North Dakota. The land was flat, so flat it looked bizarre, and grayness bathed the fields as if all color had been wrung out. Gary mentioned, in an uncharacteristically dreary tone, that his stomach hurt. I couldn't believe the magnitude of the sky and the feeling that I was riding above ground. North was all I kept thinking.

When our destination, the city of Grand Forks, appeared in the distance, it began abruptly, buildings and a water tower lined up on an edge that looked strictly formed, as if no one dared cross the boundary into the adjacent field of murky dirt. Gary took the first exit to a four-lane street loaded with stubby buildings: discount stores, gas stations, a mall, fast food. Sam's Club and Wal-Mart held central positions. Multiplex apartments, sameness upon sameness, lurked behind the main drag.

This was a city of right angles. We turned left off the east-west straight arrow of the Wal-Mart stretch onto a north-south straight arrow called Washington Street, which looked like another version of what we had just seen, only older and dirtier with trash matted in ditches along the roadside. Businesses crammed old strip malls, and new fast food chains, obnoxious islands of color, perched in front of them. Blue, red, and yellow plastic triangles at a used car dealership flapped in a strong wind coming from the west, blowing hard in the middle of town. Constant. Like ocean wind.

We found the downtown, lured toward it by the only hill—an overpass—and we rolled through slowly in our pickup, lowering the windows to let in the forty-degree springtime air. I shuddered. "Where is everyone?" We looped twice through the narrow, seemingly deserted streets lined with red brick buildings. I saw a splash of color, an awning over a vegetarian restaurant.

"That looks promising," Gary said, his mouth downturned. I put my hand on the soft hair at the back of his neck.

We'd been married two years, living in Virginia and working jobs we liked, mine as an instructor on a big campus and his as a clerk in a record store, and splitting rent three ways for a rustic house in the national forest with our friend Scott. I was the one who wanted to move to North Dakota. I was the one who had just turned thirty and wanted to do something different with my life. Gary, who'd passed thirty a couple years before without an ounce of analysis, said he loved me and would go anywhere I wanted.

Life in Virginia had been willfully uncomplicated—we worked only as much as we had to and spent our free time riding mountain bikes on forest trails or hanging out next to or in nearby Craig Creek. I taught English courses and brought home tall stacks of freshmen essays to grade, reading for self-assigned blocks of time and rewarding myself with a walk up the logging road across the highway or a plunge into the creek, which trickled over a stone dam in our backyard. Gary arranged his schedule around my teaching times and took a second job at a Roanoke coffee shop with Scott, returning home with the deep brown smell of coffee beans in his hair and hands. The winding highways of Craig County gave us time to adjust as we commuted to and from Blacksburg and Roanoke. In the early darkness of winter nights, it felt like we were going someplace deep inside as we returned to the green solitude of the Jefferson National Forest.

As my thirtieth birthday approached and then arrived—celebrated with a gourmet meal cooked by Scott and then a splash into the frigid creek, just me and Gary in our birthday suits—I wanted something different, though I wasn't certain what it was. So I did what I always do—opened the atlas and began to imagine. I applied to four graduate schools, one in Oregon, two in Alaska, and one in North Dakota. "How north should we go?" I asked Gary, after I received acceptances from Alaska and North Dakota. When we hit the road in the spring to scout out a place to rent, I told myself I made exactly the right choice. North Dakota. I couldn't wait to see it.

It was hard to get a feel for Grand Forks. We sat for a moment at an intersection near a bridge, no cars appearing from any direction to inspire us to move. I knew Minnesota lay on the other side and that the Red River of the North flowed beneath the short bridge. We couldn't see the water from where we sat in the truck, only the long, dirty decline of the embankments.

My heart felt like a lump in my chest. I knew by studying the atlas that Grand Forks would be flat, isolated, and, as I judged from the vastness of the plains and my previous experiences in South Dakota, windy. I'd been counting on the river, that winding line of promise, for beauty, for nature, which Gary and I relied on. "It's got 'Forks' in the title," he had pointed out when we studied the map together. The meandering, thick line of the Red River and the thinner line of the Red Lake River, which drained into the Red somewhere in Grand Forks, encouraged us. We liked that so many blue lines curved through the white space around Grand Forks: Sand Hill, Marsh, Wild Rice, Elm, Rush, Goose, Snake, Middle, Tamarac. I knew they'd have nothing in common with the western mountain streams I so loved or the eastern streams of Virginia. I didn't expect they'd be like the rivers in my part of Iowa, draining toward the dominant Mississippi. But, still, the Red River was a sizable stream, and we both looked forward to finding new waters.

Here we were. I hadn't noticed any water on our drive up from Fargo on I-29, and now I couldn't see anything but the bald embankments.

The afternoon gloom felt like Virginia dead winter. We didn't know what to do. The city felt strange and unwelcoming, but those vast fields beckoned to me, familiar in the way they stretched out to offer a view of the horizon. For Gary, who had spent his whole life in Virginia, Grand Forks was unlike any place he'd known. We headed west on another straight arrow of a street and continued out of town, directly toward the setting sun. The sky was all about the western horizon, so distant it felt like work for the eyes to take in, where colors were just getting started. An overpass over the interstate, which formed the western edge of Grand Forks, took us into the countryside, immediate and expansive. Gary drove a few miles until it felt like we were closer to the sun, which was lighting up horizontal clouds way out to the west in various shades of purple and orange. He turned on a dirt road that, just a few yards from the gravel we'd been driving on, rose and crossed over train tracks. We stopped short of them, got out, lowered the tailgate, and sat thigh to thigh.

I spoke first. "This isn't going to happen, is it?" This idea sat with us, its presence so tangible it seemed like another person had joined us.

Gary pulled a pint of bourbon from his backpack and poured a healthy shot into one of our plastic camping coffee mugs. We sat in silence and sipped, waiting for answers. The sun lowered into the horizon.

After a long while I said, "I could move here alone and try it out."

"I do not think I could live here." Gary lifted the mug to his lips again. I thought he might cry. He avoided looking at me and didn't even look at the sunset, which flared with spectacular color.

"I could come alone and get a roommate and just try it to see what it's like," I suggested, hoping he wouldn't agree.

"That sounds okay. I could stay in Virginia until you see how you like it and then maybe join you second semester." He said the words like he was reading a script.

He paused and continued. "How about we try it for one year? We'll consider it a tentative plan." He nodded his head once slowly, and I glanced at his darkening silhouette, the short, straight nose that made him as handsome as a hawk.

Our words were leading us and we followed, dutifully. But I also knew in unspoken ways that no matter what, I wanted to be with him. Every day. I leaned against him, felt his solid weight. We were a long, long way from Virginia, or from anywhere, it seemed.

That's when we stopped talking. In silence, we made our decision—to move to North Dakota. Made our peace with it. And this is really a true story: just as the sun went down, we decided. Hell, yes, North Dakota. "Discover the Spirit," said the state's license plates. We relinquished our national forest house, the mountains of southwest Virginia, the fresh water, the mountain bike trails, the proximity to Gary's family and our close friends, my job at Virginia Tech, Gary's job at the Record Exchange. We let go the things we loved like water, cupped into our hands, pouring through fingers. We raised a toast to the last glow of day, and the light of a train made a white circle next to where the sun disappeared. As the train approached, we put our arms around each other, and as it passed, dark, huge, and powerful, we looked into each other's eyes, and then we kissed. The ground shook.

In *Prairie Volcano*, an anthology of North Dakota writers, Martha Meek writes, "In North Dakota imagery, open spaces find their best likeness in greater space, greater vastness; we are easily moved to contemplate the universe." From that first drive up I-29, when Gary fell to silence and I reeled in thought, the open spaces of the Red River valley compelled me. I was rising higher, going north, getting close to the sky. At the same time I was afloat on a sea, the unbroken fields extending to the horizon. I didn't yet know this vast plain had once, not really so long ago, been an enormous lake. I progressed upward, becoming lighter, and at the same time progressed downward, going deeper.

Our first year in North Dakota, we lived in a place we called the Cave, a basement apartment in a house at the corner of North Sixth Street and Fourth Avenue. It hadn't been easy finding a rental in Grand Forks. The scouting trip in May turned up no opportunities; we couldn't afford much rent, and we had, heaven forbid, a *dog*, a fact that created anxiety in most potential landlords. After a series of phone calls, we agreed on the basement apartment when we found out what it would cost, $235 a month, utilities included. Pets allowed. All we really needed was a warm, dry place, somewhere to weather the winter we heard so much about. I closed my eyes and tried to picture winter in Grand Forks, but I drew a blank.

When we pulled up in front of the house in August 1995, I had two thoughts. One was that the house looked weather-beaten. A tan two-story, with a glassed-in front porch; an angled roof, barn shaped; two gables jutting out on either side at the top, like ears. Sheets of heavy plastic that moved with the breeze replaced the north-facing windows of the porch, pumping in and out unevenly, as if the house was gasping for breath.

My second thought was that I didn't know what the house was made of. What was the rough, tan outer coating? Stucco? Overgrown bushes crowded the stairs to the porch, and a row of tiger lilies permanently swayed from the wind lined the foundation. Around back, the house's coating peeled off in patches near the furnace exhaust vent, and concrete steps led down to our new rental.

In the small kitchen we found a woman whose neatly coifed blonde hair seemed mismatched to her sweatshirt and blue jeans. She fiddled with the refrigerator's broken handle.

"Hi. I'm Marlene. Welcome to North Dakota," she said, wiping her palms on her thighs. Her voice was high like a girl's. I remembered her long vowels, especially the O in North Dakota, from our phone calls. She and her husband, Robert, managed the building, which also had ground and second-floor apartments above the Cave. The owner, whose name we never learned, lived somewhere "out east," which meant anywhere east of the Mississippi River when spoken by a North Dakotan.

It took Marlene about two minutes to show us the place. We had entered through the back door, which opened into a utility room with a dusty furnace and water heater. Another door led to the kitchen, which had an undersized refrigerator and stove. The kitchen opened into the main room of the apartment, twenty by forty feet, with a front door at the foot of a narrow stairwell at one end and a bathroom at the other. The darkness and mustiness didn't surprise us, but I was unsettled by the shock of cold when I laid a hand on the wall, and the feel of the floor, hard as a parking lot, under a cheap, worn carpet. The window wells revealed a narrow view to the sky. The apartment was as we thought it would be—opposite our large house in Virginia, where the temperature inside was often the same as outside. I felt up to the challenge, purposeful in this dramatic change in our life. Rather than living in an airy house with a red tin roof surrounded by Allegheny peaks, we'd move deeper inside, living below ground—a complete opposition of places.

We gave Marlene first and last month's rent, $470 in cash, and walked up the back stairs with her. She drove off in her white Jeep with two shelties yapping at the windows. Our dog, Sam, had shifted into his violent persona, where he bared his teeth and acted as though he'd tear the shelties limb from limb, if only he could get at them. I wondered what kind of impression Marlene had gotten, after we assured her Sam was mild and would be no problem at all as a tenant. I scolded him as I removed the tie-up cord that he'd managed to wind around his legs and led him inside by the collar. He busied himself with sniffing the apartment as we unloaded the small U-Haul trailer parked outside.

Within an hour the main room of the basement apartment contained everything we owned: a mattress and box springs, a stereo and speakers, a Mac Plus computer, two folding chairs, blankets and pillows, a small TV, a VCR, books, CDs, clothes, kitchenware, a rain stick, a conga, two mountain bikes, a painting by my sister's ex-boyfriend, and a large, framed photo of a snow-covered rhododendron, given to me by a former student. In the garage we found the finishing touch, a leftover table made of thin wood supported by curling steel legs. Home, for us, was easy to situate. We slept soundly, tucked away in the deep, dark space that seemed a long way from anywhere.

The next morning I went to campus, found my office, and started introducing myself around. When I got back to the Cave at noon, Gary was on hands and knees, a box of CDs open in front of him.

"What are you doing?" I was tense. I thought he'd be out looking for work.

He read my mind. "Don't worry. I'll find a job. I just need to settle in first."

Gary and I never talked about money. We always seemed to have enough, matching our income to our lifestyle more by guesswork than by careful record keeping. My teaching income for the previous five years had been around twenty thousand dollars, and Gary earned an hourly wage from a full-time job at the record store and a part-time job at the coffee shop. When an expense arose, such as when the truck needed a new clutch, we simply went out less. When we moved in with Scott and split rent three ways, we had excess cash and traveled more often, going biking and camping, or to music shows in D.C., Richmond, or Chapel Hill. We never had a savings account. We managed to save fifteen hundred dollars before moving to North Dakota, and that had dwindled to four one-hundred-dollar bills tucked inside a novel called The Bone People.

Gary had kissed away my tears the previous summer, when I began to think about money and how we would make it in Grand Forks on my graduate assistant teaching stipend and whatever work he could find. Similar to looking for an apartment, our efforts to scout out potential jobs for Gary on our May trip had turned up nothing. When we moved to North Dakota, Gary assured me, he would make enough money for both of us.

Before Gary and I were married, I had clung to my independence like a prize, developed through cross-country moves on my own at nineteen and again at twenty-five, earning my way with scholarships, odd jobs, teaching stipends, and occasional gifts or loans from my ever-supportive parents. At twenty-seven I married Gary, but still, at thirty, I held a stubborn attitude of self-sufficiency even within the marriage when we pooled earnings. I always knew I paid my own way. Gary paid his too, though meagerly when he was in his twenties, after earning a college degree in business and finance and developing a complete, ironic lack of interest in dollars and cents. He pedaled away on his mountain bike from a job as an insurance broker, never to return. When I met him, he was twenty-seven, working at the record store where he had tried his hand at managing but asked to be demoted to clerk again, happier to be chatting about music with customers than hiring and firing employees. A mutual interest in music and a resistance to more conventional ways of settling down had brought us together, and life was seeming to work out for us in lucky, unplanned ways. We believed we could live on love.

Within two weeks in Grand Forks, Gary landed two jobs. At Menards, a home supply store on the southwest edge of town, a few blocks clear of the mall, he worked in the electrical department, selling light fixtures, ceiling fans, and bulbs. He wore a bright blue golf shirt, a tape measure, and a holstered box cutter on his belt. Nights he dealt blackjack in the lounge at the Ramada Inn for a charity called the North Dakota Association for the Disabled, part of the statewide charitable gaming network, where the maximum bet was five dollars.

Gary left the Cave five nights a week wearing a tuxedo shirt and bow tie. Hair still golden from the Virginia summer. Hazel eyes. Stocky, strong body with those mountain bike thighs inside the black pants. I wanted to crawl in his pockets and go to work with him.

Different from my moves to new places in the past, I felt pulled toward North Dakota because of its barrenness rather than the promising green of forest-land. I drove through South Dakota many times on backs and forths between my hometown in Iowa and my college town in Idaho and understood the prairie landscape only as a throughway, a place to traverse as quickly as possible on the way to the mountains or coming back home. Still, my curiosity drifted northward—if not mountains, then wide open, unpopulated spaces.

Except for one college road trip to Alberta, Grand Forks was as north as I'd ever been. I wanted to drive the back roads, drive the fields, drive east to Minnesota lake country or west to the Badlands, drive to Canada. But as we adjusted to everyday life of school and jobs, my focus came down to the immediacy of where we lived, inside the city, in our neighborhood, in our Cave, pocketed away from the vast landscape.

A few blocks southeast of our apartment, the city center carried on in its quiet way, virtually no traffic and the blocky brick buildings largely silent. I walked Sam the same route each afternoon, going toward the river, past the white house with the rosebushes out front, the crumbly apartment house with the loud music, and the plain-faced brick house with bare bulbs glaring from basement windows. A brown clapboard house coming apart at the seams always had kids banging in and out the door. The even spaces between houses and streets in our neighborhood made a grid, set parallel to the riverbank. Sam walked along proudly, white fur with one brown spot on his back, long white hair dangling from his highly held tail. His face had the markings of a St. Bernard. "What kinda dog is that?" asked the neighborhood kids, running toward us. I stepped in front of Sam, leashed him tightly behind me.

"The kind that bites," I told them, my standard line. Sam had nipped a few people over the years, and I no longer took chances. He was a fiercely loyal dog, always in gratitude, I thought, for how I rescued him from a garbage bin in Christiansburg, Virginia.

The Red River of the North, brown with the soil it washes up, ran slow and mucky at the bottom of a long, grassy slope. Sam and I wandered from the paved trail at the top and ventured down to the river's edge, a craggy, eroded rim where the exposed roots of cottonwoods knuckled the banks. The river was wide but untextured, just a flat, brown surface with muddy edges; you had to look closely to see the movement of the current. I let Sam off the leash, and he stayed out front, slowing down occasionally to let me catch up as we followed the northward flow of the river. It seemed strange—that steady, certain flow north, as if the river somehow defied gravity.

"It's a dike!" Jim McKenzie said in response to my reflections on walking the grassy slope. An American lit professor, Jim had an insistent sense of geography and a way of focusing on images that helped me begin to see my new surroundings. "The expansiveness of North Dakota will blow your mind. I'll never forget the first time I saw a train, a *whole train*, in the distance," Jim said. He told me about riding his bike in Grand Forks while the sun was low on the horizon. His shadow filled the street.

"The river floods every year, and that slope that you like so well is a dike. Haven't you noticed the water lines on the trees?" Jim lifted his hands for emphasis. Sitting in his office was becoming, for me, a way to ground myself in North Dakota. Jim was tall, broad shouldered, gray haired, and had soft green-brown eyes. Like almost every other male professor in the English Department, he had facial hair, a beautiful, wide gray moustache. "Have you noticed which one of us is clean shaven?" Jim asked, smiling with the reply in mind. "Michael Beard."

As I began my PhD studies, feeling a little resistant to being in a student desk rather than in front of the classroom, where I'd been the previous five years, Jim was the person who drew me into conversation about where I'd previously lived and what I thought about North Dakota.

"It's just hard to believe the water goes that high," I told him. The cottonwoods on the riverbank wore scars fifteen feet up their trunks, depth gauges.

"Everything is big in North Dakota terms. Big floods, big sky, big view of the prairie." Jim spoke of the variety in the landscape. The names were musical: the Drift Prairie, the Pembina Hills, the Turtle Mountains, the Missouri Breaks, the Slope, the Badlands, and the native prairie grasses, little bluestem, big bluestem, Indiangrass, blue grama, Junegrass, western wheatgrass, foxtail barley, and needle and thread.

"It's worth a trip just to see those roots," Jim said about the Manitoba Museum of Man and Nature in Winnipeg, a few hours north of Grand Forks, where an exhibit showed the curling twenty-foot roots of the original grass of the Red River valley.

"People joke about letting North Dakota go back to being a buffalo commons. The disappearance of the bison coincided with, you guessed it, white settlement. Think of those herds! Sometimes it's not that hard to picture, when you're alone, and just looking out into the prairie."

I loved that I had moved to a place where, every day, I knew where I was, could picture myself on the map. Each day brought reflection on my surroundings and what I was doing there. Gary went off to work, putting most of his time into his double jobs and taking care of us both, as he promised. I sat surrounded by books in the Fishbowl, the large reading room in the Chester Fritz library on campus, with its enormous windows and a thirty by thirty-foot layered mural—with bones at the bottom, a fox, rabbit, snake, and birds at midlevel, and a bison herd at the top. A blue stream and its tributaries floated above it all.

When I wasn't reading for my poetry and literature courses, I was reading about Grand Forks. Captain Alexander Griggs, piloting a Winnipeg-bound boat in 1870, stopped at les Grandes Fourches, a central site for nomadic Native American tribes during hunts and a stopover for fur traders and trappers. Griggs's flatboat froze in place during the night, so the captain and his men drank all the beer and liquor they had on board, and they ended up staying all winter. During this stay Griggs decided that Grand Forks should become permanent. The legend reflects the city, its love and dread of where it is. You can live in a place enticing and forbidding at the same time, and it intoxicates. At another level the legend says you'd have to be drunk to stay.

A farm river, the Red drags along with it the runoff from both Dakotas and Minnesota—potato, sugar beet, and livestock country. The water is brown and thick, meandering in bows and arcs along the North Dakota–Minnesota border. Catfish and carp troll the bottom, with only a few hatted fishermen peppering the banks, hoping for walleye. No one swims in the Red.

The city follows the meander of the river, responding to it, pushing against it, giving in. On the other side, East Grand Forks, Minnesota, does the same on a smaller scale, a town one-sixth of the size of Grand Forks, and the cities together make the midpoint of the Red River valley, like a warm spot in the plainness. The valley formed beneath an ice-dammed lake called Agassiz during the melting of the last ice age, spreading out in North Dakota, Minnesota, and Manitoba. The glacier retreated north, the lake dried, and the remaining trickle became the Red River of the North, young at ninety-three hundred years old, flowing into Lake Winnipeg. The waters of the Red mix with the waters of the Arctic, everything draining north to the land of polar bears and beluga whales.

Unlike steep river valleys, the kind I was used to, small sand hills and beach ridges form this valley's walls, which you could find if you knew what you were looking for at the outer reaches of the lake bed. The lake bed itself is rich, black sediment, and "the flattest place on earth," I heard, and I believed it. Jim McKenzie told me the flat land is still rising in rebound from the glacial weight. Still rising.

Each spring water returns to the ancient lake plain, draining from tens of thousands of square miles. Water filters into the river off the wide-open land, the natural wetlands and prairie supplanted by potatoes and sugar beets. In Fargo and Grand Forks, where there isn't much room for water, the river runs high against the dikes. Sometimes the water spills out. Spilt milk. The last time that happened and flooded the city streets was 1979.

I wanted to know North Dakota, and I especially wanted to know the Red River of the North, where it came from, how it changed, what it meant. I was born near a river, had traveled to rivers, had thrown rocks in, swum in, and drunk from rivers. I come to know myself in the way I know rivers. "Take the surface of the river between your thumb and forefinger," writes Barry Lopez. "These textures are exquisite, unexpected."

I can spend all day at a river, doing nothing more than observing the water and contemplating its presence, letting the river talk to me. In the Red River valley I found a complicated, changeable river. The annual flood was a part of the life of the river and the community, but in 1997 the river acted in ways no one had imagined. I watched as the water came up and over its banks, becoming unpredictable, and through the story of the river, I became more aware of my own life, rising into uncharted territory.

The Mississippi

The face of the water, in time, became a wonderful book—a book that was a dead language to the uneducated passenger, but which told its mind to me without reserve, delivering its most cherished secrets as clearly as if it uttered them with a voice. And it was not a book to be read once and thrown aside, for it had a new story to tell every day.

Mark Twain, *Life on the Mississippi*

I learned the Mississippi my own way as I grew up in Dubuque, Iowa, the manner it spoke, haunting the hikes I took with my father and brother, its essence present in the bluffs it had carved. The music of the *Delta Queen* paddle wheeler, with its spooky, echoing notes, reached all the way to our backyard, four miles from the river.

Lock and dam number eleven made the river as wide as a lake. Below the dam, water churned out in rapids, and the passageway of the lock held calm water at various levels, the ladder of depth lines painted on the concrete wall. Bald eagles wintered over, fishing the area below the dam. Downstream at Bellevue, lock and dam number twelve looked the same, only smaller, and my mother told how my grandpa helped build it in the 1920s and worked at a factory on the riverbank, making buttons from clam pearls. When he was older, he trolled in his aluminum boat beneath the dam for catfish.

The sloughs and islands below the Julien Dubuque Bridge, which connected Iowa and Illinois, were summertime hangouts. My friends and I used to park at the Bent Prop Marina, acting shy with our beach towels and suntan lotion, until someone offered a boat ride to Schumacher Island. We canoed Frentress Lake and rounded the peninsula, searching for herons in the jungled trees. Sometimes we hitched a ride on a boat to Nine-Mile Island at the center of the main channel and swam in the swift currents. Near downtown Dubuque we sat on the flood wall at night, the darkness of the sky meeting the darkness of the river, and slipped into the water as though slipping into a new skin.

We gathered near the Shot Tower, a monument with a history we didn't care about, where bullets were formed for the Civil War. We ignored the symbol, caught up in the intensity of our lives, when every moment felt as sharp and certain as those hot liquid lead balls that dropped and solidified, plunking into the bottom of the stone tower.

My mother warned me to stay away from the Shot Tower, the flood wall, and the train bridge, but what she really worried about was the water. She never learned to swim and feared water, hated the feel of the river and the thought that any of her children would go near it, risk themselves in the unpredictable undertows. The busy household of my youth offered me a secret freedom, however, and as the third of four children, I quietly went my own way.

The train bridge connected Iowa to the other side, the shared border of neighboring states. The Iowa side was industrial, with an old brewery and a salt factory looming, and the Wisconsin-Illinois side was a wilderness of trees surrounding the black hole of a train tunnel. The train bridge rose over the Mississippi's surface like a great machine, beckoning to us, daring us.

Summer nights hung heavy over the river, the humidity clouding so thick it was visible. When we walked on the bridge, we knew the spaces between ties weren't wide enough to slip through, but we tiptoed as though our lives depended on the careful steps, avoiding the edges, a free fall through the mist to the river.

My boyfriend Johnny was famous for his death-defying leaps off the bridge, which began with his jumping from the tracks and progressed to his clambering up the slanting bridge beams and going from the very top, a sixty-foot plunge. The summer he dropped me for another girl, I watched from the bank. I could barely see his shape through the humidity as he ascended the beam and disappeared into darkness at the top. He fell toward the water, though it was hard to distinguish in the night air, and he was only a flash, his golden blond head just a strike against the darkness. But I could hear it, we all heard it, when he hit the water, the sound echoing, amazingly loud against the rocks of the flood wall where we sat. I wanted to join him in the water, float with him as the current pulled him south and he stroked toward the bank, but he was moving in other, even more dangerous, directions.

One night when Johnny left the river in his long black Oldsmobile with the other girl in my seat, I walked out on the bridge alone. A third of the way across, I turned and inched to the edge of the ties. I took another step forward and released myself into the air. I felt the void around me, a whole empty world rising up as I fell. Then, the cold shock of water, the fight as I kept descending, too far it seemed. Finally, the forces reversed themselves and I felt myself rising and breaking through into the warm summer air. Stronger than I expected, the current pulled and the riverbank seemed a long way off. I kicked and stroked toward it, relieved when I banged into the submerged rocks of the flood wall. I crawled out, bugs biting at my ears, and found my friends, who laughed at my soaking clothes and asked where I'd been.

The water enlivened me, made me feel strong. Throughout that summer I jumped from the bridge more often, and I stopped looking for Johnny's black car.

I left Dubuque at nineteen, when Iowa had begun to feel too closed in and the Mississippi River valley too limited. After one year at the University of Northern Iowa, where I had felt a vague longing and geographical claustrophobia at the center of the state, I spent my summer with friends, drinking beer, roasting my skin on the river beaches, and languishing in the idea I was leaving Iowa. All summer I relished the bittersweet feeling of departure. While I loved the big river of my hometown, it seemed an ancient of some kind, an old, slow place that gave me a sense of security but became too safe, too familiar. As I grew and became more aware of myself, I craved the stronger, faster runoff alive with energy and color I imagined in other places. I couldn't wait to find new waters.

I spent my last night with friends on a dead-end road along the base of a bluff at the city's south end. Trees and dense brush overhung the road from the abrupt ascent of the hill. College had made me more risky, more confident. We climbed the steep incline to the levee's crest and picked our way through the riprap on the river-facing side. At the water's edge I shed my clothes, something I would never dare do in high school. My friends, also emboldened by their various college experiences, shook off their clothes, and we floated in the river together, gripping the muddy bottom with our toes to fight the current.

I bade the river goodbye and began my adulthood, when I would search landscapes with a curiosity rooted in the river valley of my home.

Two

Winter

North Dakota snows accumulate and stay the duration. Seven months of winter. Storms rolled through, one after the other, and demanded we pay attention, understand how they were lethal, even at the center of a modern city, among many people. Storms so powerful they put out the lights. So powerful they put out the heat, the water, your job. You lay in bed listening to the battering wind, wondering how the yard will look in the morning, what has blown down, when the street will be cleared, how much snow has drifted.

Ten weeks after we moved into the Cave, the first winter began. "Winter's here," Gary said, shaking snow off his coat and laughing. He'd been out getting a block heater for the truck's engine, and I was holed up, reading and listening to weather reports on the radio. After a calm, overcast morning, the gray sky suddenly unleashed the first snow in heavy diagonals. A ferocious wind came out of the northwest.

"I was afraid you wouldn't make it," I said.

"It went from autumn to winter while they worked on the truck. It's wild, isn't it? I had to kick in the four-wheel to get back." He removed his glasses and wiped steam from them.

As we had been told—*yah, you'll know it when it gits here*—the beginning of winter changed everything. Temperatures dropped to single digits and winds persisted with an arctic chill straight out of Canada. The sky took on an icy blue, and when the storms came through it seemed like curtains had been drawn, enclosing us under a low ceiling of wind and snow.

My mother-in-law, Wanda, sent money for serious parkas. Mine was forest green and zipped up over the chin to cover my mouth and nose. Protection to negative ten, the tag said. Gary went for a puffy, −40 coat that bulked him out like an astronaut. I skated my worn winter boots, lugged from place to place since I had gotten them in Idaho ten years earlier, along the ice- and snow-coated sidewalks. Around the back of our rental house, I tromped down the steps, where snow blown in by the north wind accumulated shin-deep in the concrete passageway to our basement door. Though I had been tentative at first, I found I liked living below ground level, enticed by the idea of inhabiting a place beneath the prairie landscape, where the roots of tall prairie grasses used to curl and extend like long, underground hair.

Mornings after nighttime snowstorms we heard Mark, the neighbor, running his snowblower. By the time we rose and layered ourselves in clothing, the city plow had come through and drifted our small pickup to the windows. It took a half hour to shovel the truck out from its curbside spot on Fourth Avenue because the snow was dense, compacted by the force of the plow's blades. We shoveled just enough to give the wheels some room to work, then pushed the four-wheel drive button and blasted out.

"It's like living on a glacier," I told my mother on the telephone, describing the ice and snow-packed sidewalks and streets. Cars wore dents from sliding into each other. At the airport a DC-9 skidded off an icy runway. The six-foot-ten, exuberant weatherman on a Fargo television station, Too Tall Tom, predicted days on end below zero. "We're going below the donut!" he cried.

Not wanting to drive, I took the bus. I waited on the corner wrapped head to toe in sweater, parka, gloves, hat, long underwear, jeans, wool socks, and boots, hugging my thermos. The bus driver greeted me by name and we talked about the Minnesota Vikings. Late afternoons, after returning on the bus to the empty apartment, I took Sam on his walk, regardless of weather, though at times we could go only a couple of blocks. With the deepening of winter, it became my daily challenge, and I thought, the colder, the better.

Shoveling. Shoveling. Shoveling the sidewalks, front and side of the house. Tunneling through. It felt good to shovel, and I thought I'd never get tired of it, but three storms into winter, I dreaded shoveling and envied Mark's snowblower. One night while Gary was at work, I got stuck in the street. Bound in a heavy sweater and my parka, I dug in, shoveling and chipping at ice and snow around the tires, but the truck was in to its axles. I dug out space for myself and tried to clear a spot under the truck. After twenty minutes, frustrated, ready to scream, I was spinning tires, and I couldn't get the four-wheel mechanism to engage. I got out and started digging again, and then I heard a muffled voice above me.

"Ya got cherself in a spot there, didn't cha?" came the voice through a parka snorkel, the now-familiar accent of Norwegian heritage. He looked huge above me, looming in front of the dark sky. Exhaust smoke rose out of the vehicle behind him, stopped in the middle of the road.

Without further discussion he chained our Ford Ranger to his much larger pickup and, after a few rocking tugs, lifted the tires from their snow trenches. He unhooked the chain, replaced it in the back of his truck, and continued on his way before I could thank him, his kindness another legacy of Norway. Or, as they said across the river—Minnesota Nice.

A Saturday morning in February, at negative ten degrees, Gary and I drove to Kelly's Slough, a wildlife refuge outside town, where the flatness of the landscape comes into full view. We loved the slough, wide open and full of air to breathe, sunlight to soak in, birds to contemplate. A gravel road forms a throughway between two large ponds, leading to a parking lot near the observation deck, a twenty by twenty-foot platform on eight-foot legs. The platform has stairs and a railing, looking like the decks attached to the backs of suburban houses, but at the slough it's in stark, almost comical, isolation. In winter, if you didn't know this was a refuge area, you might think there had been some mistake, that they built a deck to overlook nothing, snowy fields in every direction.

I visited with faith in the idea that nothingness can yield something, or that nothingness is something in itself. In the northern plains, is the field of vision depleted, or is it filled with something unrecognizable that might become apparent?

In deep winter the land looked utterly arctic. Ice and snow equalized the fields, and the white glare of day erased landmarks around the edges. From the platform I saw subtle, Aeolian shapes—stilled whitecaps on the open fields and drifts, exquisite in the ways they reflected sun. Long prairie grasses reached up out of the snow pack, bunched together and frozen by the wind.

With no wind at negative ten, you could walk comfortably outside if you were dressed for it, though a windless day in the North Dakota prairie was rare, especially in the expanse of Kelly's Slough. Gary and I walked across the frozen ponds, our boot steps crunching deeply into the packed snow. It was loud, crashing against the background of a wholly silent landscape.

We reached a goose nest, a wide, almost flat cone fixed on a pole. I peeked over the top and saw the most beautiful thing, a frozen goose egg. Perfect. It seemed the world was crystallized—every single detail bright and exact. Gary took a photo of me looking into the nest at the egg. You can see the individual pieces of straw in the egg's bed. You can see the rough texture of my gloves. My nose is red from the cold. Life in its details was perfectly visible.

Every day seemed an event. The girl explorer in me found new exotic territory, held still for my inspection. Coleridge's *Kubla Khan*. When I walked at the slough, loose snow blew across the frozen surface. I could see every grain.

My dreams of the north began early. Growing up in Iowa, my big brother Doug and I played Lewis and Clark, traversing forests, mountains, and ocean

beaches on the narrow, dangerous trails we imagined in the sidewalks, the backyards, and the woods behind the high school up the street. Doug and I loved winter. We dressed in layers and set out into the white world. We carved igloos out of the snow mounds our father created for us when he shoveled the driveway. Afternoons we hiked through the yard, the explorers' fighting progress through a blizzard, the distant ice cave seeming impossible to surmount, and when surmounted, crawled into with relief and delight. After heavy snowfalls we went to the high school parking lot, where the plow had pushed snow into long ridges, our mountain ranges. We climbed over them, our boots sinking in with each step. My white boot sank into a drift, and I was acutely aware of myself, savoring that feeling of being alone, in the silence of the snow, with my brother. I loved the world, the physical feeling of being in it. I loved snow, for its coldness and extremity and how it changed everything. We went home and descended to the basement, where we peeled off our snow-crusted clothes. The blue light in the furnace seemed the center of the universe.

Alaska had always seemed to me the place I would find dreams realized— what I had imagined in girlhood come to life in the landscape. I thought so not because I knew anything about Alaska, but the sound of it was thrilling. I imagined the roughness of the Alcan Highway and stopping for supplies in Whitehorse in the Yukon before continuing on the road to Fairbanks. I imagined driving north out of Fairbanks toward the Brooks Range, mountains I decided must be spectacular, spanning the high, remote arc of the state. The bays down south called to me as well, Bristol, Kuskokwim, and the Cook Inlet. I studied the locations of Soldotna, Valdez, Kodiak, and Cordova and pictured myself as a fisherman with big rubber boots and coveralls splattered in fish blood. Alaskan dreams are common. People crave that exterior, that northness and coldness. Something in us, I think, wants to push outward toward the edges, where each step takes the concentration of survival.

At thirty years old, when I moved to North Dakota, I wanted the Alaska I imagined since girlhood. I didn't expect the flat valley carved out by a glacial lake to compare to the dramatic, varied landscapes of Alaska, but I craved the internal experience of living beyond the end of the road. What I wanted in Alaska was northness, and that is what I looked for in North Dakota, not only in the white spaces of the map but in the climate—since the weather, too, is a landscape.

North meant winter. I read Jack London and hung on the words of winter, descriptions of the frozen, indomitable wilderness, the antagonistic force of the living. Life was crystallized to a kind of icy perfection, each breath significant, each step through the snow one step closer to the necessary destination—survival. Annie Dillard describes something called northing: "A kind of northing is what I wish to accomplish, a single-minded trek toward that place where any shutter left open to the zenith at night will record the wheeling of all the sky's stars as a pattern of perfect, concentric circles." In *Arctic Dreams*, Barry Lopez writes the dreamy landscape of the arctic north, where he discovers all kinds of amazing things, including that polar bears dive to the ocean floor for mussels and kelp and that there are places called polynyas, or open water, where seals, walrus, and seabirds mysteriously survive the winter.

The north is empty, sparse, and clean. Stark, barren, cold. It leaves you alone with the world.

The winter of 1996–97, our second in North Dakota, was something I'd been waiting all my life to experience, a fierce, fantastic winter. An Alaska winter. Iceland, Siberia. My imagination flared throughout a winter that just kept coming.

It began meekly, only spitting flurries throughout October, though temperatures plunged into the teens and single digits at nighttime. A more abrupt transition was coming, and we would see the beginning of winter differently because the ground-floor neighbors moved out, and we moved up. While we missed the Cave, we were glad for a change after the novelty of the cozy, dark den wore off, replaced by our awareness of mold and cramped space. Moving up to the ground floor cost us one hundred more dollars a month, earned us a weather-worn garage out back, and made us responsible for grass cutting in the summer. The apartment had a kitchen with orange counters, a living room with a fake fireplace in the corner, and bad windows, the rotting frames jammed with ill-fitting storm windows. The living room picture window, with ornamental swirls on the top section, was made of permanent double panes of glass, so thick the street, trees, and neighboring houses looked warped and blurry. The thick beige carpet made the whole place feel lucky and warm.

Sam was also glad to be above ground. In the Cave, he suffered from cabin fever, working to tunnel under the door, tearing to shreds the carpet. After we trained him to stay in a kennel when we weren't home, he seemed relieved, but it wasn't until we moved upstairs that he seemed glad to be in North Dakota, back to his old self, the smile, the wag.

The first storm came on November 16, moving in like a change of mind. Twelve inches of snow and winds of lethal temperatures and force. You don't go out during snowstorms in North Dakota, not even in the city streets. We watched the news to see what was going on, heard about cars buried in snow on the north side of town where the wind blew across Highway 2. We were making news all over, even in Iowa, where winter can be arduous. My mother mailed a photo clipped from my hometown newspaper, of a Grand Forks man at the I-29 exit to Winnipeg. The only clear images in the picture are the man's face in the wool mask, his hand on the top of the open car door, and the green interstate sign. Otherwise, the photo is white.

The Grand Forks paper named the blizzards like hurricanes, Andy, Betty, Christopher, Doris, Elmo, Franzi, Gust, and Hannah. The blizzards brought almost 100 inches of snow, more than three times the average.

During one of the blizzards in January, Franzi, I think it was, our friends Brian and Jen stopped at our apartment because they couldn't get home. They drove the mile and a half from campus at ten miles per hour, hoping not to lose traction or slide into a drift, the whiteouts so bad that Brian navigated by sense more than sight. Gary and I had been tracking reports of highway closings, even the interstate, big gates swung across the entrance ramps.

Next morning, with wind and snow still ripping the town, everything remained closed, classes at the university called off. Brian and Jen worried about their dog, Miles, who was inside their remote house, a farmstead in sugar beet country near Oslo, Minnesota. The thought of Miles trapped in the house was a constant anxiety, but, otherwise, we relaxed. I retreated to the bedroom to read. Jen lay on the futon, her head propped on a pillow, and read Michel Foucault under the snowlight coming in through the picture window. Gary and Brian dressed up and stepped outside, venturing no farther than the sidewalk in front of the house. In the late afternoon we made a meal with leftovers, including the red-skinned potatoes of local farms, creamy and almost sweet. We bided time but nothing changed; snow and wind kept on.

The second afternoon the weather eased up and we ventured into it, gusts of wind speeding and slowing our pace. We cupped our hands around our faces to see. Kicking through drifts, we followed the single set of large tire tracks down the middle of the street. I felt good inside my layers, the union suit, fleece top, jeans, parka, and all the other accessories—vest, scarf, hat, and gloves. Sam limped behind me, the pads of his feet freezing. We turned back.

Waking up to the third day of the blizzard, Brian and Jen decided to make a go of it, with us leading in the Ranger. The plows had been down the major streets, but snow filled in quickly, drifting back into the road. We passed a few other trucks, big four-by-fours with snow flying from their tires. Snowmobiles buzzed and weaved through the streets at will.

We navigated tire tracks, crossing the northernmost of the city's three bridges and turning north onto Highway 220 toward Oslo, nervous but not frightened until we got outside the city limits. Then it was like nothing I have ever seen. Everywhere, different versions of white. Snow whipped like snakes across the road—these are called finger drifts. In the distance, a yellowish white, then almost blue. Some moments—*whiteout*—you couldn't see the road, you couldn't see anything in the distance. Then the air would seem to break open and you could see solid white in the fields and grainy snow in the wind, no, not grainy, more like ribbons of snow. White everywhere, beginning just outside your eye, but sometimes you could see into the distance, the separation of wind and land.

Drifts reshaped themselves. Sunshine coming through air flashed with color, a kaleidoscope. A surreality. A nonreality. A white galaxy. Like nothing I had seen before. This was the high plains experience I had come for. It stirred the Alaska dream of childhood.

But the blizzard scared me. Gary drove, and I sat forward in the passenger seat, trying to see out the front window. During another few seconds of whiteout, I braced myself against the dash and pictured Jen's Toyota slamming into us from behind. My whole body tensed.

During a lull in the wind, we saw the highway clearly and pulled onto the shoulder, and the Toyota floated over in our wake. I shouldered the door open.

"We're going back. I don't think you should try this," I shouted to Jen, my head sticking through the rolled-down window. Heat blasted from the vents in the car.

"There are enough breaks to see. We'll be careful."

"Are you sure?"

Brian laughed, shaking his head of shaggy blond-brown hair and flashing me a smile. He had both hands on the wheel. "We'll do it for Miles!"

I told them to call when they got there. They pulled out ahead of the truck and kept going, a tiny boat in a storm, disappearing almost immediately.

They made it all the way to County Road 21, intersecting 220, where they found a ten-foot drift across the pavement. The drive back wasn't so bad, they said, because the wind died down. We fixed another meal of pasta and a can of vegetables, but our dread about Miles, going on his fourth day snowed in at the farmhouse, kept us vigilant.

"What is the worst thing that could happen?" Brian said, shrugging his shoulders beneath his thick sweater. The dog may have panicked and done a little damage to the place. So what? He was a young dog, resilient. We talked ourselves into feeling okay about Miles. He could drink from the toilet, and he wasn't going to die of starvation. We pictured Miles in the kitchen, rummaging through the cupboards. We pictured Miles opening a can of soup and pouring it into a pan. We pictured Miles doing all kinds of things and laughed at ourselves for our devotion to dogs. Sam was the center of attention, doing tricks. We cleared the kitchen table, he leapt onto it, and we applauded.

The morning broke sunny and still, the world outside so white you had to squint to see it. Snow-clearing machines rumbled down the streets, their blades pushing drifts six feet high. Brian called the highway department, finding out the gigantic drift on CR 21 was clear. He and Jen were home within a half hour.

When they pulled up in front of their house, they saw Miles in the living room window. He threw his head back and howled.

In March University of North Dakota teams won national championships in both women's basketball and men's hockey. The town buzzed with sports and with anticipation of the annual flood. When the city emergency manager called for volunteers to fill and lay sandbags on the dikes, hundreds of people showed up, with the strength of athletes, to build walls against rising water. The goals were clear—protect the city against a river that could go as high as 48 feet, as it had in 1979. A "Sand-o-meter" appeared on the front page of the paper, with graduated lines showing the number of sandbags needed. In late March almost six hundred thousand bags had been filled, and the top of the meter showed how many were needed—2.5 million.

On Friday, April 4, the Red River of the North reached flood stage, twenty-eight feet.

That same day something strange and completely unexpected happened. Though the day was lovely, almost temperate with misty air and temperatures above freezing, a blizzard watch was issued. As if on cue, the temperature fell at sunset, and the freezing mist and drizzle, which persisted with the snow, created layers of ice over everything.

When the brunt of the storm, an Alberta Clipper, crashed in from Canada, the winds snapped telephone poles and toppled radio towers. The temperature dropped thirty degrees. Gary called from the casino at the Ramada, which sat at the northwest edge of town. Fifty mile an hour sustained winds shook the whole building. Stranded travelers gathered in the motel lobby. Gary, by then the casino manager, spent long hours at the lounge and needed to be there until closing at 1:00 a.m. It was a motel, I reasoned, and if he got stranded he could get a room, but the rooms were full and people began claiming spots in the lobby, covering up with sheets, spreads, even tablecloths. Gary said he'd try to get home because things were only getting worse. Some blizzards stayed for days.

I lay on the couch, trying to lose myself in Frank Norris's naturalistic novel, *McTeague*, until the power went out, shortly after midnight. I lit candles and waited for Gary to call back. I kneeled at the double-paned picture window and watched for the lights of the truck, but the harder I looked, the less I could see. I willed Gary to find a way home through the blizzard. Something flashed, and I thought I heard an explosion, a distant, muffled boom. The wind buffeting the north side of the house grew louder, filling the room with sound.

Finally, at 2:00 a.m., I heard the familiar creak of the outer entry door. Sam knew the sound too, Gary's late-night return the only time he didn't bark at the outside door opening. Gary came in, stepping into the candlelight, his face bright with invigoration and fear. I saw someone behind him.

"That was unbelievable," he said, standing in the middle of the room in his parka and boots, covered with snow and the snow aura, as I came to think of it in North Dakota, the frigid, surrounding air pulled into a room from outside when someone entered. Bob, his coworker, followed him in, bringing along more blizzard air.

I took their coats, stiff with cold. Bob loomed in the candlelight, his large frame, his black work pants, white tuxedo shirt, black bow tie. He lived one mile away near Washington Street, but it may as well have been a hundred miles.

On their drive down Highway 2 on the north side of town, they could barely navigate in the blowing snow. Gary went in four-wheel drive, feeling his way across the same route he took home every night after work. All the lights in town were out, even the street and stoplights, but somehow they made it the mile down the highway to the turn for our neighborhood, when visibility got slightly better with the north wind behind rather than blowing across their path.

The weather could kill you. Never walk in a storm, I heard and thought overly cautionary, overly dramatic, determined as I was to experience the elements of the north. But the previous November, when a college student left a party in a blizzard, he never made it back to campus, and weeks later he was found, his body frozen to the seat of an abandoned van.

After a short night of sleep, Gary, Bob, and I woke to a cold, dark apartment, with wind and snow pounding the windows. Bob wore his tuxedo shirt and black pants, too shy to accept our offer of other clothes and hoping he would be able to get home soon. We sat in the kitchen listening to KFGO in Fargo, the only station coming through the static on the transistor radio. A voice hollowed out with the long vowels of North Dakota told of winds and temperatures that were hard to believe, one gust at negative ninety-nine, they said. They aired telephone calls from people asking for help, looking for those who were missing—*please, please call and let us know you're okay*. One caller warned people to be careful with candles, she didn't know what to do, she wanted everyone to know the danger, she didn't know how we'd get through it, because the night before she lost her house to a fire. Someone gave instructions on how to reverse an energy flow with a portable generator to get electricity, and another called to say don't do it—you'll fry the linemen out there working. The voices crackled into our kitchen.

Gary, Bob, and I stayed for hours at the table, listening to the radio, staying warm under blankets. In the afternoon, when the storm eased, the phone calls changed, became lighter. People gave and asked for advice: build a tent in the living room to make it fun for the kids while you try to keep them warm. If you're cold, take a warm pet to bed with you. "When is the storm going to end?" someone asked the radio announcer.

"At seventeen minutes after the hour." Which hour?

Announcer: "I don't know!"

Emergency shelters opened in the Civic Center and at schools. News reports gave descriptions of incredible accidents, such as a car in a water-filled ditch, the ambulance getting stuck on its way, then the wrecker sent to get the ambulance getting stuck. Finally, two people with hypothermia were rescued from the car along with a third person who swam through slushy, frigid water to an abandoned house.

Gary and I went outside in the afternoon, safe inside our layers, the sun a shadow behind the snowy air. In the stilled downtown we saw stuck cars, drifts formed over them. Suddenly a moving car came around the corner, sliding crazily through the street, smashing into drifts and backing up and accelerating again. The young men inside, cramming the car full, shouted and laughed.

In our yard we found a limping sparrow. We took it inside, put it in a box, and gave it a pan of seed and water. It sputtered a little and perched on the edge of the pan. When movement started coming back to its wings, we let it out the back door and watched it fly to a treetop.

The storm blew out late Sunday, and in the sunlight of Monday morning, Gary and I drove Bob to his small blue truck in the Ramada parking lot. Bob yanked on the frozen door, and on the third tug it opened with a loud creak. The truck made no sound, not even a click, when he tried starting it. He raised the hood to find solid snow, only the air filter peeking out. Bob crowded back into the Ranger's small front seat, and we drove him home, skidding around in the smooth places left by plows. We walked him to his apartment door and hugged him goodbye as if completing a long journey.

Blizzards made me feel my place in the world. I could see myself from above, a dot on the map at the top of North Dakota, snuggled into a pinpoint in the

midst of white space. Winter erased the surroundings and made an empty expanse, the place-beyond-the-end-of-the-road I had always dreamed of finding.
It felt like self-diminishment, shrinking beneath the power of much greater,
humbling forces, and I was left alone with words and images, burrowing into
our apartment.

At the same time, when the weather blew in, I wanted to go outside. We had
to be careful in the winds and temperatures under negative twenty-five, which
had instant freezing power. I took Sam out, where all winter he used a corner
of the yard, his own pit toilet dug in the snow. Even though I ran him, trying to
keep him warm, his legs cramped, stopping in midair. I rubbed his hips to get
the blood flowing, and he ran in circles. On the way back in, he stopped on the
sidewalk and bit wildly at the pads of his frozen paws. One time, after both of
his haunches seemed to be freezing, I lugged his forty-five-pound body to my
chest and carried him in.

My desire to live remotely goes as far back as I can remember, but it is
bound by a paradox: while I want to live away, I don't want to be alone. The
excitement of the blizzards had as much to do with the phenomenal wind and
snowfall as the pleasure of being with friends and with Gary, inside and safe.

When Gary came through the door, wrapped in the snow aura, I wanted
to bring him inside and take care of him, feeling together the struggle of us
against the world. Gary, Bob, and I stayed up until almost dawn, wrapped in
quilts and talking in the candlelight. The storms brought out this intimacy,
where we folded into each other. Outside, the world became a landscape of
nothingness, everything erased and leaving us to ourselves, safe and warm
souls waiting inside the storm.

August in Iowa, ninety-five degrees and you're dripping with sweat the moment you step outside. My father drives me west out of Dubuque in the family car, a silver Monte Carlo with no air conditioning, and by the time we arrive at our destination, a central Iowa farm, my right arm is sunburned from where I was swimming it through the air out my open window.

My father shakes hands with the parents of Val, a girl I met only one time before, when the National Student Exchange office arranged our shared ride. I packed my laundry basket of clean, folded clothes and duffel bag of books and shoes into the back of Val's Chevette, waved to my father going the other direction, and Val and I set out. We stopped at Iowa's north border, where she took my photo near the Minnesota-shaped "Welcome to Minnesota" sign, and at Minneapolis, we caught I-94, angling up the long northwestern diagonal, heading into the sun.

St. Cloud. Alexandria. Fergus Falls. Beyond Fergus Falls, so much of what you see is land and sky, nothing else, no signs of the Midwest. Farms, trees, antennae, fences, and water towers disappeared. Iowa faded behind as we drove into the promise of more emptiness, more vast western landscapes. More sky than land in view. As we approached Fargo, the land abruptly flattened, as though it had been sheared off into one enormous plain. Flatness is nothingness, many people think, but this kind of flatness was like opening a window on the sky.

I studied the map as Val drove, tracking our location, picturing myself from above, going west. I felt buoyant, staring out the car window for hours, content to be taken wherever we might go, the farther from familiar territory, the better.

Val, a pretty girl with curly black hair, light blue eyes, and a Scarlett O'Hara pucker, spoke about the West in mythical terms. "You will not believe what you're seeing," she told me. "Wait until we get to the mountains." She told of her family's trips out west, how high elevations take your breath away, how mountain roads make you feel you're going up when you're really going down. Val had no intention of stopping until we got to the place she knew as the

West, beginning in the middle of Montana. We passed sunflower fields, their gold capturing a whole day's worth of sunlight, and rode into the line of the horizon.

Watching the sun set over the western expanse, I thought of the landscape as beautifully complex and simple at once, where everything seems in view and close to the earth, and what is unseen is holding up the sky.

I returned to Iowa after my exchange program, but I couldn't stop thinking of Idaho. I transferred to the University of Idaho at the beginning of my junior year, and the trip from Iowa to Idaho each autumn and spring became a regular rhythm in my life, an interim for me to make the switch. I was strongly identified with both places. Idaho, with its astounding, mountainous landscapes, liberated me from my past, the landscape of Iowa that had almost no wilderness, most of the land used up in farming. When I went home, I returned to my taproot, remembering the richness of the soil and the old familiar river. I rejoined my family, bringing stories of the West.

The speed of the perennial trips out and back depended on how quickly I got through the Dakotas, the landlocked region that didn't seem worth stopping for. South Dakota was the usual route, with its dubious promises of the Corn Palace and Wall Drug. The only certain stop was the overlook at Chamberlain, where the Missouri River cut through and made a decisive split between the green farm fields to the east and the arid, brown hills to the west. The river marked the transition between the Midwest and West, a symbolism I focused on, often with tears, as I made my passages to and from those landscapes.

The North Dakota route, the road less traveled, offered a giant bison statue—the "World's Largest Buffalo"—at Jamestown and a remarkable, sudden entry to the North Dakota Badlands, where, depending on the sunlight, you found layers of warm colors making it look as though you gazed into a wide, colorful yawn of the earth.

Traveling the Dakotas was a matter of getting through, of going somewhere else. I never stopped to think about what I missed.

In 1987 I rode with a dozen other students two hours south of the university in Moscow, Idaho, into the Salmon River Canyon, where, at a small town called Riggins with khaki mountains rising up at steep angles, we boarded two rafts and set out into the river. The mountains were amazingly dry and bald, the river amazingly green and deep. The most simple landscape, as well as a place of sudden change, the river becoming rough at the rapids, the mountains transforming around each bend. My companions knew the place—they told me about the river current, the rocky hazards, and the white sands where we'd camp.

All day we rode north on the current, interrupted by occasional wide, frothy rapids that bumped and tumbled us around, though the big raft rode them well. Cold at the start, we heated up as the sun beat down from a spot exactly centered above the canyon, and we peeled our wetsuits like layers of skin. One of my new friends showed me how to roll out of the raft and ride in the water with my arms wrapped around my life vest and my feet extended out front. These waters, making a sharp turn at Riggins after descending from the green depths of the River of No Return Wilderness, were wild and unbound, cutting through a landscape with a beauty I had dreamed.

We would leave the water before it met the even larger waters of the Snake, running parallel only ten miles to the west in Hell's Canyon. I laid my head back in the cool stream, so recently come down out of the mountains. I felt my life was just beginning, my understanding of the world opening wide.

The Snake, the Salmon, the Clearwater, and the Selway—those western rivers I came to know during my college years in Idaho—matched my visions of perfect water.

Three The Flood Fight

Some time when the river is ice ask me
mistakes I have made. Ask me whether
what I have done is my life.
                    "Ask Me," William Stafford

The Red River valley flood season began with predictions, and 1997 told of an extremely high river to come. The deep snows, still frozen, promised some sort of transformation, but we didn't know what to expect. The previous spring the river rose against the dikes, its swift current revealed by icebergs and broken tree limbs traveling north. Outside town Gary and I cruised country roads between flooded fields. Even though we knew the water wasn't deep, and in a month tractors would chug through the black gumbo in the same spaces, we relished the sparkling waters as if they were lakes. I drove while Gary scanned from the passenger seat, binoculars ready. Beavers motored through waterways, bald eagles fished, and migrating waterfowl floated, friendly brigades bobbing on the windy surface.

I pondered the dividing lines of appearance and reality, lakes taking the place of the unbroken whiteness I got to know in winter, those oceanic expanses. The fields of the Red River valley had looked like an inland sea, wind-blasted shapes formed in the snow, like still shots of whitewater. In spring we lived somewhere different, the inland sea becoming the lake country we envied in our neighbor, Minnesota, the land of more than ten thousand lakes.

The great malleability of the Red River valley, changeable by season. Arctic tundra, cool lakes, croplands.

Four years into my marriage, I understood how our love of landscapes had brought us together. Gary and I fell in love by exploring, by driving in the truck on Virginia back roads, scanning the land, soaking up silence and soil and air and texture. We communicated without words, knowing we had met another person with the ability to cut loose from routine and cross boundaries into the wilderness. We found the roads leading outward and stopped to make love in the forest, places in the wide open where it was just us, our bodies, and the land. *I feel like myself*, we'd often say on our escapes into the natural world.

Moving to North Dakota was a risk, a detachment from the places we loved mutually and where we found our stride together. While I inspected the surroundings with a curiosity built up in my years living out west, Gary, who would've never moved away from Virginia if it weren't for me, had more trouble connecting with the massive sky, incredible flatness, and lack of shape. We no longer shared a sense of landscape.

We confronted the surroundings together. We complained to each other about the smell when the wind was wrong and brought aromas of the french fry factory in Grand Forks or the sugar beet–processing plant and sludge ponds in East Grand Forks. After giving up on the tiny, easy mountain bike loop at Turtle River State Park, we bought street tires and rode on country highways, finding pedaling into the wind more difficult than climbing mountains in Virginia. We faced the weather as a challenge, walking outside on subzero days, ducking into doorways downtown to catch our breath during wind gusts with chill factors below negative fifty.

The harsh winter and the coming of the big flood in 1997 enticed and dared us, a newly found way to experience North Dakota.

I dreamed last night of a big flood coming. The ocean was rising. Some beautiful images including the huge moon coming up over the water. The water was like a mirror. And the waves were coming fast. Journal entry, mid-March

When Blizzard Hannah cleared out, the weather turned—snow dissolved and the sun gained momentum. Only days after we huddled under blankets in the apartment, I walked the neighborhood in lighter layers, a sweatshirt and jeans.

Except for a few patches in March, the grass had been mantled by snow since the previous autumn. Now the melt was on, revealing winter-traumatized yards, brown, matted grass looking dead and beyond hope. It was hard to imagine the reappearance of green. Trees held their winter look, no promise of budding. But with the sun coming on stronger, we hoped for the undertaking of the new season, early, this year.

The river rose. Water surpassed the flood stains on the cottonwoods on the greenway where I walked Sam, but the water had room to rise, the long slope available for spillover. In other parts of town, water rose more insistently against the dikes.

South of Grand Forks, strange things were happening. At Breckenridge, Minnesota, where the Red River originated with the confluence of the Bois de Sioux and the Otter Tail rivers, the flooding rivers filled the streets and froze, forming large sheets of ice. At Ada, Minnesota, the Wild Rice and Marsh rivers, tributaries of the Red, crashed into town after an ice jam wrecked a levee. The National Guard used boats to rescue people from the wall of water, then the flood stopped in the streets like Venice frozen over. Enormous chunks of ice had to be chopped up and hauled away.

At Fargo the Wild Rice and Sheyenne rivers overflowed their banks. As those waters joined with the Red running between Fargo and Moorhead, Minnesota, everyone watched, the water tunneling through a space that seemed much too small, but aside from the overflow into one neighborhood, the dikes held. Vice President Al Gore showed up to give encouragement and throw ceremonial sandbags. The river topped out at 37.5 feet, more than 20 feet above flood stage and close to its height of 1979, Fargo's worst flood ever.

North of Fargo, free of the constricting dikes, the water expanded, grew to more than ten miles wide. We heard there was a slow-moving lake coming north.

Our life revolved around numbers—dates, flood levels, and sandbag totals. The highest water level ever recorded in Grand Forks was 48.8 feet, in 1979. In 1997 we could expect a huge flood, with the National Weather Service predicting the Red to crest at 50 feet during the third week of April. Flooding had already begun, soaking buildings and homes and closing the Point Bridge, the southernmost of three bridges adjoining Grand Forks and East Grand Forks. During the second week of April, the Sorlie Bridge closed, leaving only the Kennedy with its high span. The bridge symbolized movement and connection between North Dakota and Minnesota, and on a deeper level, it symbolized control.

We were sandbagging. Like crazy. Gary and I wore designated flood fight clothes. He donned an old gray jacket, one I had teased him about, saying it washed out his natural color, though I loved the jacket because it reminded me of Virginia and our early days when the grayness should have made him blend in but somehow made him stand out in a crowd. I wore a lightweight blue parka, another leftover from Idaho retrieved from the back of the closet. We had knee-high rubber boots, recent purchases for the occasion, and an array of gloves and stocking hats, waiting warm, dry, and ready on the radiator in our apartment. I enjoyed wearing my gray toboggan hat so that I didn't have to wash or comb my short, straight brown hair.

The Public Works building on the west side of town was renamed Sandbag Central. On the large floor of the main building, two sandbag-filling machines had been assembled, and all day, every day, volunteers gathered around the sixty-foot-high, steel contraptions, like enormous spiders with stiff legs.

Conveyor belts transported sand from truck beds, a steady stream rising and dumping into the big bucket at the top of the machine. The bucket rotated and released spurts of sand down diagonal chutes, the spider's legs, just enough to fill a sandbag. At the bottom a person caught the sand in a bag. Sandbags were burlap or tightly woven white plastic. The sand catcher passed to the next person, who twisted the empty neck of the bag. The twister handed off to a person who bent a thick, U-shaped wire around the neck and tightened it with a special tool that looked like a crocheting needle. Six people stood in each sandbag line extending out from the legs of the spider, so at a machine with eight chutes, forty-eight workers filled thousands of sandbags every hour.

I liked using the binding tool. I bent the wire around the neck of the sandbag, inserted the needle in the loop, and jerked it tight. Then I swung the bag behind me and laid it on a conveyor belt, where it rode to the hands of other workers who stacked the bags on pallets in the back of a truck. The symphony of sound—the trucks beeping as they backed up, the banging on the chutes to loosen clogged sand, the roar of motors—swirled around and infused my body with the rhythms of work.

The work felt real and immediate. True. I loved collaborating with strangers, the feeling of hands synchronized at their various tasks.

Big trucks rolled across the cold floor, loaded with the effects of our labor, and made deliveries at the river, where more lines of people stacked the bags atop the dikes. My hands roughened, my eyes quickened, and my hips and back muscled up. After a few hours of work, I felt I'd really done something.

Everyone watched or imagined the river, compelled by its current, its force, its threat. In filling sandbags, we worked to save the town and everyone in it. Sandbags were our mission.

Massive amounts of water were coming. The gauge for worry had been forty-nine feet, the level nearly reached in the flood of 1979. During the second week of April, the words "Get Ready for 50 Feet" appeared in big black letters on the newspaper's front page. Schools and businesses closed so that people could join the sandbag lines. At the university only about half the students showed up to classes. Water swelled in the English Coulee and leaked into two fraternities and a dining hall.

Some of the students cared, some didn't. "I've never really felt like I'm a part of Grand Forks. It's like the university is one town and Grand Forks is another," said Shawn, a student in my writing class. Others nodded in agreement.

Kristen shook her head. "I think that if you live somewhere, you should help take care of it." I liked that idea, but I was keeping quiet.

"I skip most classes to go out and help. I mean, how can we just sit around when the water is going into people's houses?" said Molli, shaking her head of white-blonde Norwegian hair. I remembered her poem from the week before at a reading at a downtown coffee shop, citing the threat of high water. Images of the swollen river and the watery farm fields rose to the top in their stories and poems.

Younger, which student would I have been? Living a variety of places has brought me a sense of responsibility, but when I was younger, I worked so hard at defining myself that I wasn't much aware of how I might take part in a community.

Some of the students got out and joined the city, and others went their own way. I could see myself in both.

April 16. Over a million sandbags raised the height of the dikes. The Red River exceeded 49 feet, and people began saying it was the flood of the century. The National Weather Service changed the crest prediction to 50.5 feet. The city engineer said the dikes would hold against 52 feet of water. But there was talk of evacuation. If the river went over 50 feet, we'd be in *unknown territory,* the mayor said.

Friday, April 18, 2:00 a.m.
Like apparitions on a wet black bough. That's how the faces looked, peering out the bus windows at those of us waiting to board. The faces in the windows, the school bus, the city street—everything—was vaguely illuminated by yellow streetlights. The air hung heavy with the feel of the river. One at a time, we stepped into the ghostly bus as if we were beginning a journey to the underworld.

Gary and I swung into a seat, and I pressed my forehead to the cold glass of the window. Every moment, every sensation recorded itself on me, became detailed into my memory. Since midnight, when Gary came home from work with news that people were out on the dikes, working through the night, I had been alert, ready for action. Another part of my mind, the quiet, observant part, wanted to memorize, measure, and record each moment.

Everyone wore their battle clothes, familiar to us now after a month of working in Sandbag Central and on the dikes. Parkas streaked with mud, big brown rubber boots or Sorels, hats of all shapes and sizes, dirty gloves. My own clothes were stiff, having dried on the radiator after my earlier shift of filling sandbags.

The inside of the bus was brighter than I expected, too bright, revealing the strain and weariness in people's faces. I leaned into Gary's shoulder. He discussed the evacuation with a man sitting next to him, how Lincoln Park had been cleared out after a dike sprung a leak. The leak was repaired, but no one could go back, and all the houses in the neighborhood stood empty, closed up. I tried to picture the broad clay dike springing a leak. I saw the river pouring through a hole, and someone sticking a finger in to stop it.

The bus rolled to Lincoln Park. Enormous white beams shot out of two round bases as large as tractor tires and illuminated the hillside, which looked unnaturally bright, lit up like a movie set. The ring dike, the steepest in town, rose above the houses in a grassy slope, fifty feet high. A long, snaking line of people ascended the dike from the bottom, where pallets of sandbags were forklifted from the back of a dump truck. At the top of the dike, a horizontal line of people passed sandbags one to the next. I couldn't see what happened at the end of the line, where sandbags seemed to disappear into the darkness.

When our bus came into view, the line dismantled, people slipping and sliding down the hill. They rushed the bus, pushing in before we got out. When I stepped out, it felt as if the ground might give under my feet.

Holding hands, Gary and I turned our feet sideways and dug in. Slipping, we fell to our knees and rebalanced with our hands, crawling to the top. There, I saw the most astonishing thing, the image I've come back to over and over—how the black, fast river had topped the earthen dike to the level of the sandbags and lapped against them. Gary, I, and all these people teetered on a dangerous edge.

It was a feeling before an image as my eyes focused, and I saw into the darkness. The river, usually a sedate stream you could ignore thirty feet below, was only an arm's length away. Kneeling, we could have plunged our hands in. The people, awkwardly swinging sandbags from one to the next, could have misstepped and fallen in, or the water could have burst through the bags. There would have been no getting out. I couldn't believe the speed of the river. To my left the top branches of a submerged tree whipped violently in the current. Large icebergs cruised past. The bluish reflection of the floodlights showed a river that looked a mile wide.

While we had seen its quick ascent in our own neighborhood, gentle because of the expansiveness of the dike, we hadn't been aware of the river's drastic rise in this part of town. The surface roiled with the blackness of ink. It seemed as if the earth had opened up and revealed its primitive depths, where water took command. I felt I was standing at the edge of the world looking down, looking deep.

Gary and I joined in the process by filling gaps on the sandbag line at the top. At first the bags came rapidly, and Gary loaded each into my arms. I swiveled and delivered bags to my left until ten minutes later, when the bags stopped ascending. At the bottom, people gathered behind the empty dump truck. Pallets, cleared of their sandbag piles, tumbled around like wreckage.

I heard a scream below me. A boy in a letter jacket skidded his boots down the muddy hillside and fell to his knees at the bottom. Two girls followed. The group got up, shook themselves out, and climbed up for another turn. Someone shouted at them and said to get down. Get the hell off the dike.

When others began to leave the sandbag line, Gary took my hand, and we sidestepped the hill, avoiding long streaks of mud. At the Red Cross trailer at street level, we asked for coffee, and the woman inside the trailer offered us something to go with it. Cookies. Apples. "Eat something! You need the energy." I felt safe again, relieved to be off the top of the dike. We smiled at people around us, chatted with them about the height of the dike. With the voices all around, next to the bright trailer, an optimism filled me, a desire to keep working in the company of the other flood workers. It went beyond optimism too—a bright desire to fight off what threatened.

"They must be out of sandbags," said a guy in a muddy parka and a UND ball cap, emerging from the darkness behind the trailer. He spoke in a loud voice so all of us could hear.

"I doubt we'll see any more trucks tonight."

"Okay with me. I gotta get back home and keep at it," said another man, wearing a sweatshirt and a bomber hat with fur lining, the loose flaps swaying under his chin as he spoke. "I got three feeta sandbags around the back of my house."

Gary spoke softly to me. "Maybe we should get on the next bus." He had both his gloved hands wrapped around the foam cup.

"I don't know. I won't be able to sleep if we go home."

"Well, maybe we could go somewhere else and work." Gary set his coffee on the ground, took my freezing hand, which I was trying to warm by blowing into it, and placed it inside his coat, beneath his arm.

The Red had risen to almost 51 feet that afternoon, and the crest projection changed to 51.5. Tonight was the night, it seemed, the river might top out.

"I don't even want to go in," I told Gary after we returned to the Civic Center on the bus and walked the three blocks to our apartment. The neighborhood held still under a misty, dark cloak. I knew that if we went inside, I would take off my layers of clothes and lie down. The night air was cold and enlivening, and my mind reeled with the sight of the river at Lincoln Park. I wanted to be near the river, watch it rise. I didn't want to miss anything.

I squeezed Gary's hand. "What do you think?"

"Yeah. I'm game. I'm sure there's something we could be doing."

At home we passed the front door and went to the garage, where we got into the truck and switched on the radio. The emergency broadcast, as it had been for days, was giving instructions. "East Grand Forks needs people to fill sandbags. Anyone who can help, please go to the parking lot behind McDonalds on Highway 220." It was 4:00 a.m. A few other cars and trucks moved along the city streets with us, navigating the uncertainties.

"Do you think the bridge will stay open?" I said to Gary.

"I don't know. The mayor said so, but I don't know."

"Should we cross?"

"I think it'll be all right." Gary was calm, though I knew from his eyes that he felt as I did—nerves zapping with every thought and feeling. When I blinked, I saw flashes of brightness, the combination of exhaustion and energy playing tricks in my body. I felt buoyant riding down Fifth Street, talking about what might happen as if it was a fascinating idea, a distant possibility. My fears were just beneath the surface, bobbing up but not recognizable in the swift current of thought.

And so what if we couldn't get back? The dog was at home, closed into his kennel. I tried to think of what in the apartment I couldn't bear to lose— like that old English teacher's journal assignment: if your house was burning down, what would you take out with you at the last minute? *The fire*, I once heard. But this was real life. What would I take? The dog. The computer. Nothing else came to mind. Over the years Gary had kept a blue backpack, a small bag filled with his personal things. The letters I wrote when we were falling in love in Virginia. A box of fishing lures. Lists of CDs to add to his collection. Pens. Pocketknives. Miniature flashlights. Photos. Birthday cards. A torn, muddy piece of paper with the number 227, which he'd worn on his back in his first mountain bike race. Reminders of his life. But reminders had never seemed as important as the life we were living, the present moment our most valued possession.

But there was Sam. If they closed the bridge, we reasoned, we'd have to drive eighty miles south to Fargo and loop back through North Dakota to get to Sam. That wouldn't be so bad. We could do that, Gary said quietly, nodding. His assuredness made me feel relieved.

Ours was the only vehicle on the Kennedy Bridge, and we slowed down to get a look at the river. I rolled down the window and strained to see, hanging my arms over the door. It was too dark. I couldn't see how high the water was.

In East Grand Forks a hundred people gathered around a sandbag-filling machine, the same kind we had worked on at Sandbag Central. The East Grand Forks mayor had issued a challenge to raise the dikes—*two feet in two days.* When asked if we knew what to do, we said yes and took the place of two people who looked bug-eyed.

The pace was frantic. Someone asked where we were from. "Grand Forks," I shouted above the fray.

"Did they wake you up too?" My puzzled look urged him to continue, a wild-eyed man with orange hair. He wrung the neck of a sandbag and spun the bulk of it with his free hand. Between twists, he reached up and pushed his glasses higher on his nose. "The cops. Did they wake you up over there?"

He described how East Grand Forks police cars drove up and down streets, blasting their sirens. "Come out and help if you want to save your neighborhood!" the man said, mimicking the sound of a voice in a bullhorn. He looked like Gene Wilder, and I stifled a laugh.

Loop the wire around, insert the crocheting needle, pull tight. Pass the sandbag to Gary, who lays it on the conveyor belt. No time for thought, but I get lost in a kind of white-thought, my mind as automatic as my hands.

"Are you doing okay?" said Gary. I nodded. More silent work. "Still okay?" Yes.

I smiled at him and gestured with my head toward my back. It ached, but I wasn't ready to quit.

We continued for an hour, passing bags one to the next until my body felt detached from my mind, hands automatically carrying out the assigned task. The twenty-five-pound sandbags felt as light as small bags of sugar. No one spoke, but we communicated, passing hand to hand, filling a truck bed.

Then something broke my rhythm. I looked down to see fingers squeezing my shoulder.

A tall, slender man in camouflage, flat hat pulled down on his brow and pants tucked into boots, pulled me gently backward. I stepped aside as another camo-clad person took Gary's place. All around us, soldiers filled in at the sandbag machine.

I felt I had just been awakened. "Looks like our replacements are here," Gary said. He paused. "Maybe we should go home." In the east, clouds brightened.

"There's a bus leaving to lay bags on the dike," I said, repeating what I heard as others left the sandbagging machine and wondered what to do next. Aimlessly, we walked toward the street. In the distance, we heard sirens.

"How long have those been going off?"

"I don't know," Gary replied. "I just noticed them too."

"Let's go home."

We drove slowly over the bridge, the black river only a few feet below. The water seemed to levitate, hanging beneath the bridge. Water risen up out of its natural bed, flowing north, rising into the air.

You like to take risks, my mother once said. I had left out a lot in our conversations over the years, but still, my mother seemed to know. Roads I'd driven in Idaho, high elevations, looking off into the vast, seemingly bottomless valleys and canyons as I drove the red truck that she and my father had generously supplied me. Camping alone with my dog in Idaho and Montana. Getting into cold water at night, the world disappearing as I swam into a void, then returning to land, grateful for the feel of something solid under my feet. I was unlike my mother, a person who so loves her roots in eastern Iowa that she feels uncomfortable leaving home, even for a day. I liked testing boundaries, seeing where the world changed and became something completely different, unexpected.

The flood in Grand Forks was enormous, far bigger than anything we'd imagined. Crossing the bridge back to North Dakota, we understood new things were coming.

My Waters
Virginia

Moving from place to place forms me, changes me, shows me how to live. Sometimes I can hardly believe what I've seen. At my first view of the mountains, when I was nineteen, I refused to believe in them, seeing them as storm clouds on the western horizon. When I got close enough to touch a mountain—in Glacier National Park—I was astonished to find I could reach an arm out and place a hand flat against the incline.

Going to college in Idaho gave me my grounding, and I spun off from there, driving my small red pickup, using any excuse to travel favorite highways in Idaho, Montana, Washington, and Oregon. Memory is a map of place and experience. The hot springs on Lolo Pass, the spray from Multnomah Falls, Mount Rainier suddenly appearing through clouds, the mosquito attack near Craters of the Moon, the unlikely chorus of moos in the Owyhee Desert. Out west I marveled at the available beauty, the everyday occurrence of extraordinary land, all of it lit by a clear, absolute sunlight.

The day I left Moscow, Idaho, I packed all I had in the back of my Chevy s-10 and hit Highway 95 south, taking a last glimpse of my college town in the rearview mirror. Many miles after Moscow disappeared into its soft pocket of Palouse farmland, I saw the mountain ridge behind me, the dark green double hump of Twin Buttes and the higher point of Moscow Mountain. The mountains had come to symbolize the available wilderness of Idaho, places I traveled for camping and hiking trips, enveloped by evergreen canopies that made me feel a million miles from anywhere and right at home at the same time. It was the smell as much as the feeling of being on those green mountainsides that intoxicated me.

I hated to leave Idaho but was compelled away by a desire to know other places. I had thrived in the idea I was sequestered, alone in the frontier, the high-elevation hills of the Palouse with its shiny, wavering wheat, a landscape that seems to be brighter because it's closer to the sun. But I knew it was time to go after I finished bachelor's and master's degrees, and I matched job advertisements and maps, searching for patches of green. I had never been to Virginia, or anywhere near it, when I accepted a job there.

A steamy July day, a few weeks after I left Idaho, I exited an interstate that wound through the hills of West Virginia, and for a short stretch followed a clear, rocky creek and eased onto Highway 460 toward Blacksburg, Virginia. The mountains were low and long, the trees puffy and green, like broccoli. I kept feeling on the verge of wilderness but not reaching it, especially when I passed a worn-out power plant with a smokestack rising like an enormous middle finger flipping off the surroundings. Even while I came to love those mountains, I never forgot the first glimpse, and I had to learn to negotiate the network of back roads, zeroing in on pockets of wilderness. The New River, said to be one of the oldest rivers in the world, wound through the mountains near Blacksburg. It was a bold, strange river with glistening rapids, black pools, and foamy runoff. Everything I learned out west seemed turned over and around by Appalachian perspectives.

At the corner of Faculty and Progress streets, I took a downtown apartment with cavernous rooms. To stop the echoes, I fastened blankets on the walls and hauled in thrift shop furniture. I kept my pet, a black and white, nameless lop-eared rabbit, in a large cage in the corner, occasionally letting him out to hop across the wooden floors.

The Record Exchange, a store up the street, is where I met Gary, who had sandy, messy hair, light green eyes, and a wardrobe of shorts and T-shirts emblazoned with band names and labels such as Sub Pop records, Basehead, African Rubber Dub, and Funkadelic—"Free your mind and your ass will follow." We saw each other out in the clubs, where we attended the same kinds of music shows, Buffalo Tom, the Blake Babies, Tiny Lights, American Music Club, and Uncle Tupelo.

I knew I'd met a soul mate the first time Gary and I visited a stream together. On Poverty Creek at the base of Brush Mountain outside Blacksburg, we slipped off big slabs of granite into the spring runoff and scrambled back out, hooting about the icy temperature, and then sat together with our legs outstretched, skin standing up beneath the cold droplets of water. The sun did its work to dry us. We stayed for hours, getting back in when we were dry and hot, and then out again for the cycle of sunbathing. Under the same spell, the waters enlivening us, and the sun, the sun that seemed so enormous it took up the whole sky over the valley, fortifying our skin. If the sun stayed uncovered and never left the top of the sky, we'd ask no questions and stay forever.

Gary helped me get to know the streams of southwest Virginia, especially Craig Creek, the eastern continental divide, where we waded, collected fossils, and made love on the banks. Farther downstream where the water deepened, we went fishing and tubing on stretches of the creek he had known since he was a boy. Gary took me to the James and the Jackson, his two favorite rivers, and told stories twenty years old about particular fish, how the water felt, what the weather was like, what it felt like to bring the fish in, to release them. He also told about being on the rivers as he got older, the friends he paddled with, what they ate and drank, how they floated hours and hours, sometimes until after dark.

I constantly put words to the test, delivering love letters to Gary, slipping them into his pocket at the record store or folding them into his bike frame, retelling the marvelous days we spent together. My letters tried to tell Gary about how he looked in the water and sunlight and how I felt about him, but the paragraphs became descriptions of Virginia, the rivers and streams. My love for the landscape and my love for Gary were deeply entwined.

On a snowy February day on the banks of Craig Creek, standing next to a bonfire, we got married. Mr. Burk, the clerk of court for our county—who fished the creek and knew the stretch we described—agreed to drive out and meet us and thirty of our friends and family. All day we stood around the fire, sipped champagne and beer, and threw stones in the water. At two in the afternoon, we had a ceremony with our friends reading passages from philosophy and poetry. I read a poem I wrote the night before about how the waters east of the creek flowed toward Gary's river, the James, and the waters west of the creek flowed toward mine, the Mississippi. When everyone else left the meadow, promising to meet us later for a party, Gary and I walked the creek, checking fossils and dipping our hands into the cold, low winter waters that held so many promises for the fullness of spring.

The summer after we married, Gary and I moved from one rental to a smaller, cozier rental one block west on Kabrich Street in Blacksburg. The small tan house lost its exterior paint in curling peels to reveal planks of old yellow pine. We borrowed a small hand sander, paint scrapers, and brushes and proceeded clockwise, scraping and sanding, using butter knives to get at the uneven surfaces of the warping wood. We rotated the sander in small, loving circles as a finishing touch. "We're massaging the whole house," I told Gary.

The house seemed one big bedroom as we draped ourselves over the two flowered couches that Gary's mother gave us or flopped onto the mattress and box springs surrounded by piles of discarded clothing. I gave Gary massages, proceeding up and down his body with the pressing of fingers made strong by house painting. It seemed we were always lying down at that house—resting, sleeping, making love. When we weren't due at work on campus or at the record store, we mounted our bikes and rode loops through the mountain valleys on roads like Catawba, Mount Tabor, Dry Run, and Shadow Lake, our knobby tires purring with the friction of pavement. On days we didn't have to work at all, we drove to the mountains and biked the trails.

The following summer Scott, Gary's best friend from high school, invited us to share the rent on his house in Craig County, an Appalachian two-story with a wood-burning stove, a red tin roof, and Craig Creek running through the backyard. With Scott, we kept very little in the one-hundred-year-old house, called the Hancock House, just the essentials—bikes, music, books. The ground floor featured a picnic set already there when Scott moved in, a table and two movable benches covered with a thick, shiny shellac. We put Gary's couches on the screened-in porch facing the creek, and whole afternoons could be spent lying down, listening to water. With one small push mower, we shared grass cutting, so much lawn to take care of that the mowing never ended. Gary and Scott showed me the trails in the national forest where they ran mountain bike races in the late eighties. We also rode trails Gary learned from his father, a native of Craig County: the Arm Trail on Potts Mountain; the jeep trail on Bald Mountain; the Deer, Grouse, and Turkey trails on North Mountain; and the trail on the backbone of Patterson Mountain. We cut wood for our stove, collected water from a spring on Bald, and swam in the creek. Gary caught perch, smallmouth bass, and chain pickerel in deep, black holes, and I wrote poems, though daydreaming often took over. I watched all the birds come and go, the usual suspects—robins, nuthatches, chickadees, and goldfinches. There was a kingfisher I called my personal friend.

In winter we spent most days at our jobs in Roanoke and Blacksburg, and the house darkened early. Without a fire in the woodstove, the temperature was nearly the same inside as out. We gathered at the shellacked table for late evening gourmet meals fixed by Scott and got to know red wines. In a small empty room upstairs, we hooked up a TV and VCR to watch movies rented from the log cabin store up the road, the few dramas we could find among wrestling and hunting videos.

In spring, when Craig Creek flooded, we watched it transform the banks, washing away the stone fire circle and pebbled beach. The water came within a foot of the prized deck affixed above the bank, a large sturdy square set there by the previous renters, who had won it in a raffle. Gary and Scott leaned over the railing of the deck, watching the water rage by, and I stood farther back, afraid to get closer, afraid the water could tear them away. The water roared as loudly as Idaho rapids, though it tumbled gray and ominous, unlike the western waters that look so at home, snowy white between the high walls of green or brown mountainsides. Here it seemed water rose against its own will, the vegetation on the banks jerked and torn violently. The water became our focus, and all bike riding, gourmet meals, and music sessions ended while we sat out back, waiting to see what the water would do.

That spring it flooded some houses down the road from us, where people had prepared by moving their furniture to higher ground. Otherwise, the creek's rising did nothing more than thrill and entertain us. When it fell to regular levels again, we missed the surprises, like the refrigerator that had floated by, and most of all we missed the sound.

After Gary and I moved to North Dakota, Scott remained in the house, and the following spring, when another flood rose, it came even higher. Scott said when the deck was torn away, it drifted calmly and intact, looking as if it was going elsewhere to reattach itself, to give someone else a view.

Four Evacuation

Gary and I couldn't see the orb of the rising sun as we drove home from East Grand Forks after the all-night rush to fill sandbags and build dikes, but we saw its light pinkening the bottoms of the cloud layers in the east. The top of the sky began as light blue, promising a clear, maybe even warm day.

Later we would talk about how the color of dawn infused the sky as we walked from the garage toward the house, and, it seemed, saturated the air surrounding us. The wail of the siren came in waves, loud, fading a bit, then loud again. Colors and sound melted together.

"Is that siren for our neighborhood?" My way of asking if we should be afraid.

"I don't know. I'm not even thinking about it. I just want to lay down a while." Gary's shoulders drooped. He opened the back door to let Sam out, and I took to the damp grass and listened to the sirens. The breaking of day seemed to release us from duty somehow, the blue sky a sign that we needed to stop the frantic work, get some sleep. Others would take over. I wasn't sure what the sirens meant or how long they'd been blaring.

We weren't sure what was happening, how or where or if the flooding would continue. All I knew was that we were safe in our house; the river in our part of town—so flat, with the long, gradual slope down to the riverbank—wasn't going to come crashing through any dikes. But the siren sounded so close, the same one that had scared us a year before while we played tennis on a court seven blocks away and had to sprint home on our bike pedals. Massive storm clouds had reconfigured themselves, making a shelf of ominous black bubbles over us, looking as if they might at any moment release a funnel cloud.

The sirens were strange, swirling in the clear air, at the breaking of a beautiful day.

Gary held a transistor to his ear. "They're evacuating Riverside this morning." He gestured with his chin toward the neighborhood a mile northwest. I didn't understand. One part of my mind imagined the steep dike at Riverside, the water pouring over in an even, beautiful flow, like a waterfall. Another part saw the water held back behind the top of the dike, people forced to leave out of some kind of fear, irrationality, or overcompensation. Also, I pictured people staying in bed, waiting for the sirens to stop so they could get back to sleep. We'd been through a month of emergencies.

"It's not like the water is just going to go crashing over, right?"

"I think the dikes could start leaking. Maybe they want to get people out before anything happens." He stood up, stretched, called Sam back.

"No classes again today," he added.

The usual immediacy of sirens—their sudden, alarming blare—dissolved in the wider transformations: the look of the river, people on the streets all night, the military reinforcements taking over the town. Gary and I went inside to get some rest. In bed we pressed our nude bodies together, trying to warm our damp, waterlogged skin. I felt Gary's tired muscles jerk during his quick descent into sleep, then his slow, measured breathing at my neck. I slid from his grip, lay on my back, and tried to relax by beginning at my feet, imagining each part of my body as separate, floating. When I got to my lower back, I realized I was holding breath at the top of my chest, as if trying to stay buoyant in water. I let the breath out and felt myself sinking into a warm liquid, saturating my body and swirling around my bones, detaching them, submerging them. The room darkened, black as the river.

Loud knocks came from downstairs. I slid my bare feet into the tall, cold rubber boots standing ready in their usual spot outside the front door and walked downstairs.

The door of the Cave stood open. "Hello?"

"In here," someone called from the bathroom. I found our landlady on hands and knees.

"Should we move Josh's things upstairs?" she asked, speaking to me over her shoulder, her hands working a large wrench at the base of the toilet. Josh, who'd moved into the Cave during the previous autumn, was in Montana for his grandmother's funeral.

"What's going on?" I asked. Marlene sat on her heels, running the back of a hand across her forehead. She told me she was going to move the toilet off its base and plug the sewage pipes because the city's system could get backed up.

"I don't think Josh would like it too well if things overflowed here," she said, turning back to her work with a giggle. "Is Gary around? Maybe he can help me move this toilet," she said matter-of-factly. She had strong hands, like a man's, and a youthful face, far younger looking than her fifty-something years. She wore dirty jeans and a collared shirt that looked as though it had just been ironed.

"You might want to think about moving Josh's things upstairs. This house's never had water in it, but who knows what's going to happen." Marlene sounded tentative, but I was glad to be given something to do.

I went upstairs, woke Gary, changed clothes, and returned to begin taking some of Josh's things up the stairs to stack in our living room. Pillows, lamp, shoes. Videos. Josh was working on a master's in film—he'd need those. I looked through the kitchen. Pots and pans? I didn't see the point of taking everything up.

When Gary and Marlene finished their work, we stood with hands on hips in the middle of the Cave. Marlene straightened her glasses with a delicate touch on each side of the frame.

"Did you hear about Lincoln Park?" she asked. The ring dike, illuminated by the big white lights, jumped into my mind.

"The dikes are leaking and water is in the streets."

"Have you been over there, Marlene?" Gary asked. He gripped the back of his neck and rolled his head, giving himself a quick massage.

"I heard about it on the radio. They got everyone out in the middle of the night." Marlene frowned, but then giggled again, nervously.

"This house has never been wet, but who's sure about anything anymore?" She shrugged and smiled at us, then scooped a pile of clothing out of Josh's dresser. She stopped in the doorway and looked back at us over her shoulder.

"If you have to leave, make sure to turn off the main breaker and gas."

We thanked her and swung into action again, clearing out the dresser. We heard Sam's barking upstairs as Marlene stepped into our living room to add the clothes to the accumulating pile.

Gary smiled at me. "Let's pick up the pace."

Up went the television. Boxes of books. Hangers of shirts and pants. With each trip up the narrow stairwell, its one curve sharp and difficult to maneuver, we were silent but thinking the same thing—the river water couldn't possibly reach this house.

Midmorning. We sat on our bed and considered what to take if we had to leave. The sirens had stopped, but radio reports told of neighborhood evacuations. Riverside Park, Central Park, Belmont. Schools and businesses closed. Families could go to the Grand Forks Air Base for food and shelter or call the Emergency Operations Center for help. The mayor's voice sounded steady but urgent, like the radio voices during the blizzards.

Gary perched on the edge of the bed, contemplating a pair of sweat socks. "I think we should leave. Let's go down to Hastings. We can come back on Monday. Things ought to be calmed down by then." For months we'd been planning a trip to Hastings, Minnesota, to celebrate my birthday and see my parents, who were driving up from Iowa. It was Gary's first weekend off in months, and he wasn't due back at the casino until Monday evening.

I thought we should stay, dig in. Our refrigerator and cupboards were stocked with food. I wanted to see what the river would do. "How about a motel room on the other side of town?" I suggested as a compromise.

"I don't know. I think we should go." Gary stood up, picked a shirt and sweatshirt from the closet.

Fresh air, rising water, the exertion of muscles along muscles, lines of people swinging sandbags one to the next—I didn't want to give up the flood fight.

"Let's go see your family and come back ready to work," he said. We weren't giving up on the flood fight, he told me. We were just taking a break.

It was the sun, finally, that persuaded me. I looked out the window at the bright light, full force and climbing toward the top of the sky. This might be the first day of real spring.

Spring days in North Dakota were spectacular after you lived through a lethal winter. New life, indeed, with all the sunshine and warm temperatures. Typically, spring didn't get going with any serious duration until May, but sometimes April days shined through, sun blasts dividing the low, overcast sky. Sixty degrees in North Dakota in April felt like a heat wave. The blue sky, air so clear it feels good to breathe, the temperature just right, no humidity, and the breeze carrying a coolness like mountain water.

After we decided to go to Minnesota, Gary left in the truck to make the casino's bank deposit, as he did almost every morning, and I hooked a leash to Sam so that we could take one last look at the river. Sam and I took our regular route, Fourth Avenue, walking down the middle of the street, no traffic, as usual. The cross streets, usually more alive with traffic, were empty this morning, and a spooky quietness pervaded the neighborhood. Perhaps we were the last to go. I wondered about the families on my street, if they were driving to the air base. It seemed strange that no one was outside. Even the house with the loud kids and dogs stood silent.

I hadn't seen the river along our usual walking route for a couple of days. I crossed Third, climbed the short incline to the paved bike path along the dike's crest, and stopped cold. I could hardly believe what I was seeing. The water had risen almost to the top, covering the enormous field that I had come to know through our walks. The big old cottonwoods were submerged to their highest branches, and the river had completely swallowed the small trees and bushes higher up on the bank.

The water looked still and calm, one huge, ugly puddle.

Sam and I walked toward the old train bridge, where a group of people in camouflage worked, piling up sandbags. Their heads turned all at once.

"This neighborhood's been evacuated." One guy stepped to the front, looking nervous and official. He looked as though he was going to salute me.

"We're just on our way out," I said and paused, studying them. They looked exactly the same, pants tucked into black boots and flat-topped hats shadowing their faces.

Upriver, at the closed Sorlie Bridge, Humvees were parked on both sides, facing out, and more people in camouflage worked on sandbag dikes. I felt usurped—my days as a soldier taken over by real soldiers. I envied their mission.

I couldn't stop thinking about what was in our apartment, what might be lost to the floodwaters, even while I didn't believe anything was going to happen. I phoned my friend and teacher Elizabeth, who lived a mile and a half west of the river, and asked to store my computer at her house. "I won't be here and the house will be locked," she said. "But go ahead and put it in the garage if it makes you feel better." After I hung up I felt embarrassed, thinking I was overreacting. We'd be back in a couple of days. Still, when Gary returned from the bank, I asked him to help me lift the computer to the top shelf of a closet.

Golf clubs, overnight bags, and my birthday cake, the special butterscotch kind my mother-in-law sent ingredients for every year. Gary went upstairs to tell the neighbor we'd be back Sunday night and to turn off the main breaker switch and gas if she had to leave. She said she wasn't going anywhere.

"Here we go, evacuating," Gary said as we walked behind the house. He had the golf clubs strapped over a shoulder, and he held the cake pan up on his flattened palm, like a waiter.

On the Kennedy Bridge Gary slowed almost to a stop. The current was huge, littered with moving objects: logs, plastic jugs, lumber. A hot-water heater? Cottonwood branches lurched. On the Minnesota side, a backhoe stood motionless though precariously balanced, it seemed, and one small line of people worked on a sandbag dike. The water looked propped up, held high by the dikes on both sides.

Sam was to stay with Brian and Jen, as he usually did when we went out of town. We took Minnesota 220 north, the same highway where we'd been caught in the surrealistic ground blizzard the previous winter. What we saw was a shock. Water everywhere. The road appeared stretched, wavering on top of a lake.

"Is it just because I'm tired, or is this totally bizarre?" Gary's eyes were wide. I reached over and squeezed the back of his neck. Everything seemed to be in movement, the white-capped fields shimmering and the truck shaking in the wind.

Water, water, every where, And all the boards did shrink; Water, water, every where, Nor any drop to drink. The flood, for us, had been limited to the riverbed in town, where the water rose in its narrow path. We hadn't considered what was going on out in the countryside. "What is this? River water?" I couldn't make sense of what I was seeing.

Gary made the turn for Brian and Jen's place, steadying the truck on the narrow brown lane, the only available land. Logically, we knew the water could be only one or two feet deep, but it felt like we were guiding the truck on an edge, and falling off would mean total submersion. The yellow house and all that surrounded it—the outbuildings and junked car collection of their landlord—was dry, perched on an island.

"Oh my God, that's unbelievable. Have you driven out there?" I called to Brian and Jen as we pulled up and got out. They were sitting on the front step, sharing a cigarette, a choke, as they called it.

"Yeah, isn't it something?" I was glad to see Brian's calm demeanor, his perpetual smile.

"What about you guys? Is this place safe?" Gary asked, his eyes squinting with concern.

It was the high water table, they said, holding runoff in the fields. The floodwaters of the Red were safely distant, a half-mile to the west. Their dog, Miles, and Sam chased each other through the yard at full speed. We sat on the steps, taking in the sunshine and looking out at the lake view. I dreaded the drive back out the lane, whitecaps whipped up on open water in places that should have contained safe, dense dirt, places where sugar beets and potatoes grow.

"We're just going to wait it out. The water has to start going down soon," Jen said. She twisted the end of the cigarette into the concrete of the front porch, her straight brown hair falling in front of her face.

"We'd better get going." Gary stood up, stretched, called Sam over to say goodbye. I hugged Brian and Jen and wished them luck, feeling reassured by their steadiness, their willingness to stay.

Gary drove the flooded roadway while I clutched the door handle, my heart thumping, listening to the tires roll across the narrow tracks. When we made it back onto the main highway, I rested my head against the seat and closed my eyes. We headed east on Highway 2 to south 59, toward Mahnomen on the White Earth Reservation, listening to radio broadcasts from Grand Forks. The seven-step evacuation process was reduced to two: secure where you live by plugging drains and turning off the main breaker and gas, and get out. The mayor's voice crackled and eventually faded. When we stopped hearing her voice, it was like a door slammed shut.

This was a landscape we had come to love, where the Red River valley gives way to hills, forests, and lakes. On Highway 59 we weren't far from Itasca State Park, where we made pilgrimages to the headwaters of the Mississippi.

My face in the rearview mirror looked odd, swollen under the eyes, and I shook my head, trying to wake my brain. I felt underwater. On Sunday we'd return and get back to work.

My brother Charlie and his wife, Sue, lived in a three-bedroom house on a quiet street in Hastings, an old Mississippi River town downstream from St. Paul. After living in the Uptown neighborhood of Minneapolis for five years, where they went out to see live music, had parties, and worked on master's degrees in education, they moved a half hour outside the Twin Cities and took teaching jobs in a big high school.

Even when I lived far away from Charlie, we remained close, calling each other every week and spending time together in the summer at home in Iowa, where we went swimming in the river, drank beer, and drove to Ames and Iowa City to see our favorite bands like the Gear Daddies and the Flaming Lips. He accompanied me back and forth on my drives between college and home—I taught him how to camp and he taught me about music. We would leave Iowa on a beeline for the Black Hills, blaring Hüsker Dü, our long hair flying out the rolled-down windows of my Chevy s-10 truck, and we pitched tents wherever we could after we ran out of sunlight. One year we ended up at the Harley Davidson rally at Sturgis, South Dakota, staying up all night with the bikers, sharing the case of Star beer we'd brought from home, a gritty beer made in an old brewery on the riverbank. Made with river water, we always said.

"We'll be neighbors," he'd said when I called to say Gary and I were moving to North Dakota. The six-hour drive became a regular event, Gary and I going south, or Charlie and Sue coming to Grand Forks. They always made it up for the Potato Bowl in September, when we'd attend the University of North Dakota football game, smuggling small bottles of bourbon or Schnapps in our coats, and afterward stuffing ourselves with the free potatoes offered in bars and restaurants around town. We shared a love for the rich, red-skinned Red River valley potatoes, which we found in the city streets during harvest, bounced out of truck beds. "Like food fell from the sky," Charlie said.

"I just don't feel right," I said to Gary as we turned off the freeway to the connecting highway to Hastings. I tilted the rearview mirror toward me. My face looked different, swollen. Flooding on the inside.

"I'm just glad to be here." Gary sat straight up, gripped the wheel, stretched out his lower back.

At Charlie's, a note on the front door read, "Gone to Wal-Mart. Beer in Fridge." We pushed open the door, dumped our bags in the foyer, picked up the beers, and headed for the back porch. The lilac bushes lining the backyard were on the verge of blooming, and the sky was Minnesota blue, bright in the evening. We sat slumped in lawn chairs, faces turned upward, taking in the fragrance of the new grass and the last of the sun.

An hour later they burst in. Sue was eight months pregnant and looking fantastic in an old flannel shirt and stretch pants, my brother following closely. Next came my parents, laughing and talking as they walked toward us, my mother opening her arms and saying, "They're here," and hugging us both at once. My dad stood to the side, waiting his turn. We circled the chairs on the porch.

Gary told about the previous night on the dike and in East Grand Forks, moving Josh's things, seeing the flooded fields, and dropping off Sam. I added details. We spoke of our plans to return to Grand Forks on Sunday.

I pictured us: hip boots; heavy, waterproof coats, like firefighters; big, tough gloves, the kind I wore to throw sandbags. Throwing sandbags. I loved the sound of that, the toughness of the verb, the knowledge of their weight. What would it take to fight the flood?

We talked until dark and then went up the street to the Biersteube tavern, where we drank more beer, ate hamburgers, and kept talking. Words flowed in and out, like water. My mind worked in flashes, from the lit hillside of the dike at Lincoln Park, to the poster in the dormitory window reading "Build the Ark," to the backhoe balancing on the dike in East Grand Forks. My mother noticed my flood face, the swelling under my eyes. She took my hand and told me she was glad we drove down.

At midnight Gary and I lay down in my brother's guest room and stretched out on our backs. My body was already relaxed, the muscles feeling disconnected.

I closed my eyes and pictured North Dakota from above, as I had seen it from airplane windows. In winter the whiteness is almost complete. Except for buildings, roads, and lines of trees, you see nothing but white. In the warm months you see the patchwork of the large, flat farms and their various shades of soil. In both seasons—warm and cold—the Red River is the most identifiable thing down there, meandering in tight spirals, narrow lines of trees on both sides outlining the river.

The floodwater was rising outside those lines and spilling into the squares, making a broad, expansive lake. Lake Agassiz, the Pleistocene glacial lake that formed the valley, had returned, a ghost haunting from the past.

When I drifted off, I had visions. Scenes of raging, rising water.

The Dubuque Flood

April 1965. Heavy late winter snows in Minnesota and northern Wisconsin begin melting, and the Mississippi rises. The people of Dubuque listen and watch as the crest moves southward, the swell of the river approaching the city, and dike work begins in earnest. Thirteen-foot-thick earthen dikes are formed, snaking more than three miles along the river's edge.

Of the two bridges in town, the upper bridge, connecting Dubuque to rural Wisconsin, closes. The lower, main bridge, connecting downtown Dubuque to East Dubuque, Illinois, is kept open, with volunteer sandbaggers working to protect the ramp from the floodwaters on inundated Locust Street. Schools and businesses close as people join in the flood fight. In all, more than four hundred thousand sandbags are used to hold off the river.

April 20, the night of my birth. My father is not at the hospital. He is down at the river, throwing sandbags on the dike with the players and other coaches of his high school football team. At 3:00 a.m., I slide wet and sleek from my mother's body.

Early on the twenty-fourth a fire breaks out in Standard Brands Egg Plant. Firefighters go by boat to battle the blaze, which is a half-mile from dry land. The fire is extinguished before it can spread to other buildings.

A storm pounds the dikes the night before the river crests, with twenty mile per hour winds battering workers who pump water from behind the dikes. Though some water seeps through, the dikes hold when the river crests at 26.8 feet on April 26, just after midnight.

No one dies in the flood, but it changes Dubuque. Damage estimates are near 10 million dollars. The city lobbies for federal money to help in building a flood wall for future protection, and the massive project is begun a few years later, eventually costing 4.5 million dollars. The system of levees, made from sand and clay of the Mississippi basin, stretches five miles along the riverfront, guarding a town that would never see the river the same way again.

The flood of April 1965 was the biggest in Dubuque's history, and it coincided with my entry to the world. "Your birthday makes me think of floods," my father recently told me, reminding me of how I was born from water into water.

Five The Ghost of Lake Agassiz

I woke to a small sound, a distant phone ringing, raised my head to the window, and looked into the dim light of early morning. Checked the sky, my daily habit, but I couldn't yet see if it was blue or overcast. The bedroom door, opening slowly, scraped the carpet, and I heard my sister-in-law Sue's whisper.

"Jane. Phone."

Sue retreated to the shadows behind the half-open door of her bedroom across the hall, and I descended the stairs to the phone in the kitchen, the knowledge that something was wrong compelling me forward, the prospect of disaster frightening and exciting me.

"Have you heard, Jane?" It was Jen.

"No. What?"

And I'll never forget what she said. "The whole town went under. Grand Forks is completely gone."

Strange words. The town gone? The dikes were breaking, Jen said, and water was flooding the entire city. I leaned against the kitchen counter, looked out the small window next to the pantry. In the twilight the lilac bushes made a dark, definitive line between the yards. I thought of the bridge and the river, water pushing against the banks and piles of sandbags—how easy it was to imagine the river pouring over.

At some level I had already imagined it. What Jen told me was like a review of something that already happened, a story already told. Water spread smooth and expansive, like the opening of hands. But her words were stunning in their scope, paradoxical in that they were expected while being a complete surprise.

Still, the immediate. The practical. Jen's voice sounded strong and certain. She and Brian needed to leave their house in the country, she said. Water closing in. "We're not really scared. Not yet. But who knows what's going to happen next?"

"Get out of there as soon as possible. *Go*," I told her.

"We'll go as soon as we finish packing. I'm looking forward to getting away from all this water." Brian had readied his Volvo with camping gear and supplies, and they'd leave within the hour for a campground in central

Minnesota. Dogs in the backseat—the kids. We laughed. She and Brian were okay, she assured me.

"The road out seems to be dry."

"Seems to be?" The Volvo could tip, be submerged in the surrounding lake.

"No, really, Brian checked it. The water isn't any higher here today."

The water in the fields surrounding their home held the usual spring runoff, deep this year because of heavy winter snows. What didn't seem possible was actually happening—their fields were taking on water from the Red River, a half-mile to the west, which was expanding uncontrollably. *A lake, ten miles across, moving north*—as the flood was described in the Fargo newspaper. That description stayed with me, gave me an image for what was happening in the Red River valley. The lake had reached Grand Forks and Brian and Jen's home. When they left, they'd be driving across water, looking for shore.

When we first moved to North Dakota, the flatness of the landscape amazed us, a flatness so complete that it went beyond a characteristic and became a thing, a subject matter, an event. One of my professors, Martha Meek, says that when people first encounter the flatness, it either silences them or they can't stop talking about it. "The prairie seems to require a counterforce: an explosion, an interruption of human energy and will," she writes in *Prairie Volcano*.

The geological story helped me see and understand the flatness. Through the wavering summer heat or the crystallizing lens of winter air, I could perceive the old bed of ancient Lake Agassiz. On sojourns to the countryside, Gary and I eventually found the small sandy hills indicating the lake's east and west reaches. The landscape made sense with the image of the lake.

So now—the flood. The reminiscence of a valley. The return of the glacial lake. The ghost of Lake Agassiz.

After the phone call the house returned to its sleeping silence, eerie now. In the bedroom I found Gary, usually a sound sleeper, lying stiffly on his back, eyes wide open. I sat down on the bed and took his hand. He pulled me in beside him and I told him what Jen said. "Oh my God, really?" He sat up and swung his feet to the floor. "Let's go turn on the news," he said, something I hadn't thought of doing.

It was a strange anticipation. Following the record-setting blizzards and the monthlong flood fight with more than a million sandbags and twenty-four-hour dike patrols, the next event seemed the inevitable climax. I wanted something to happen, all that water to do something, mean something. Working on the dikes, we must've known—hadn't we?—that we couldn't hold off the enormous river.

Aerial shot. Water pours over the ring dike at Lincoln Park, the same ridge where we piled sandbags twenty-eight hours before. The flow is shiny and robust, like a long, uniform waterfall. The sandbags hold beneath the water, magnified by its lens.

Water pours over the ledge of the dike, and I think of hidden wing dams on the Mississippi. Water cascades down the long slope, smooth, like hair, I think, or cloth. The camera switches to street level. Only rooftops.

Aerial shot. Downtown looks much larger than it really is. Rows of square building tops—were there really that many buildings in downtown Grand Forks? Camera angle switches to water halfway up the doors and windows. The street is replaced by the water, a new, higher surface. A small tree struggles and shakes in the current.

Switch channels. More aerial shots, this time houses with identical roofs. The camera drops down—helicopter shots—showing how water has reached the eaves. A band of A-shaped roofs line up, treetops bushing up among them. I wonder if the houses will uproot and float. Or crash into one another. Or be covered by water. The reporter's voice crackles, backed by the thwap thwap of helicopter blades. He says half the town is flooded.

Who are these people in hip waders, standing in our streets with microphones? I envy their proximity—I crave the experience of being near all the water we waited for. I wanted to stand in it as they were, feel the push of the current.

Here is an NBC reporter on Washington Street, a half-mile from our house and the river. With water to his knees. What about our neighborhood? How deep had the water gone? If it was knee deep on Washington, it must be waist deep or higher where we lived. Water rose halfway up the doors of the buildings downtown. How could there possibly be this much water?

Our minds go back and forth, testing possibilities. We are held back, watching the television screen, waiting for imagery of what is damaged and lost. The water floods our sense of the familiar, damages our sense of the permanent, and still we watch with an expectation, as yet unspoken, to return and reclaim.

Anticipation, fear, arousal. Heightened awareness of where we are, what we have. When the river takes over, everything we know goes into transformation.

We witness the force of Earth and experience, and we can only wait and see what happens.

All morning we watch, snuggling into a pink afghan in my brother's TV room and clutching cups of coffee. Lenny, my brother's dachshund, curls in behind me on the oversized plaid couch, rests his skinny nose on top of my hip. I'm grateful for the slow rise and fall of his little body.

Sixty percent of Grand Forks and all of East Grand Forks are flooded. Massive sections of the cities are evacuated, though some people can't get out, and boats and Humvees sent in by the federal government go to their rescue. Vehicles roll through the flooded streets, tires spraying water and making waves, to dry passage on the west and south sides of town. The lines of traffic look epic in their meaning, people driving away with belongings stuffed into and tied on top of sagging cars.

Thousands go to the Grand Forks air base, fifteen miles west of town, to hangars organized with cots and food distribution. The University of North Dakota calls off classes for the semester. Storm sewers back up. The flood-water is four feet deep in downtown Grand Forks. Hundreds of houses are submerged to the eaves, and thousands more have water rising in their base-ments and on ground level. The water plant fails, creating a paradox in the crisis: too much water spoils the water. Along with fresh water, all the other basics—fuel, electricity, and food—are gone, leaving most of the city breaking down beneath a wide, muddy, poisoned stream.

Gary and I huddle on the couch. I don't know if I should huddle in farther or get up off the couch. And do something.

When the news reports become repetitive, I get determined, picturing myself and Gary piling back into the Ranger and heading north. I want to be in the flood, as that reporter was. Could I navigate the waters back to our apartment? Our small apartment, so full of nothing, yet carefully arranged with the things of our life. The hand-me-downs in the living room—including the frayed chair and rickety bookshelves left by the former tenants. Expendable. The futon my parents gave us, its mattress slumping from constant use. The stereo, like any stereo, replaceable. The thirteen-inch television I bought with a boyfriend ten years earlier in Idaho, a boyfriend I would like to forget. Good riddance.

My desk was made of cinder blocks and one sturdy piece of wood, three feet by two feet, with gray and blue fabric pinned on by Gary. The bedroom held a box spring and mattress on the floor—no frame—headed by a heavy shelf Gary found in an alley. Even while loaded with the appliances we loved using—waffle iron, coffee grinder, and food chopper—the kitchen didn't have anything irreplaceable. Go ahead, wash it away. It would prove what I liked to think about Gary's and my life, that it was so simplified we were perfectly mobile. Happiness on wheels.

But, wait. There was more. Photos and journals. Our treasured mountain bikes, both the Specialized brand, mine a Rockhopper and Gary's a Stumpjumper. All my books and Gary's music. How important? My books had been carefully chosen over the years; I kept only a minimum, not the typical habit of an English teacher and graduate student. Occasionally I moved a book out of the collection, finding it a different home and replacing it with a newcomer so that the only books on my shelves were those that made the cut, that remained essential to my life and way of seeing the world. Sometimes that way of seeing shifted, and with it, the book collection shifted.

And then there was Gary's music. Away from our common ground of the natural world, we were drawn together by our love of music. But our tastes were different. With five hundred CDs in our apartment, people had asked me before, "What kind of music does Gary like?" I couldn't answer. His tastes were eclectic, subversive, unpredictable. Sometimes, away from the apartment for a while, I returned to find a CD in the player, something with an unpronounceable name.

"What's this?" I'd ask.

"Bobatunde Olatunji," he replied. It was taken from his lineup, somewhere between African Head Charge and Hector Zazou. Of his hundreds of CDs, I had listened to maybe fifty. We gave each other a wide berth, mine from Gary's music, his from my poetry.

How easily could Gary leave it all behind? They were just things, after all. Grand Forks was gone—and maybe this was a sign for us to leave, take advantage of a cleanly wiped slate and start again. Two thoughts ballooned. Go back and save what was left, reclaim our place. The other thought was that we'd let go of it all, relinquish it and be cleansed, free to begin again, anywhere. How many times could I start over?

At midday nothing seemed to be changing. My parents, brother, and sister-in-law left for the afternoon, sensing we needed some time alone. As soon as they were gone, we knew what we needed to do, the thought occurring suddenly and mutually. We headed for the phone.

We couldn't reach anyone, our friends' numbers dead-ending in endless rings or fast busy signals, but when Gary called the offices of Northern Lights Public Radio, where he did a Sunday morning eclectic music show, someone answered.

"Hey, who's this?" Gary sounded abrupt. I leaned in and we shared the phone receiver.

I could hear someone speaking loudly. Gary pressed the phone closer to his ear, trying to understand the person on the other end.

"What?" he asked and then held the phone away, studying it in his hand. He shrugged and replaced it on the cradle.

"He hung up," he said. "I heard something about taking a canoe out to save the transmitter."

"Wow." I paused. "This is all so strange."

Gary put his arms around me. All morning we'd been touching, sitting close on the couch, and now he faced me and gave his familiar, wide hug, his encompassing chest and arms taking me in. "Let's go outside for a while, okay? Look at that sunshine out there."

The day was perfect, Minnesota-styled springtime with a sun brightly contrasting the blue sky. We took blankets and pillows to the back patio, positioning ourselves so we faced the light. I was glad to feel the heat and wanted it to burn—burn out the waterlogged feeling of my head. The thoughts gathered at the back of my mind began to disperse, and my whole body lightened, felt as though it was lifting into the sky.

By the time everyone came back, Gary and I were on our feet, putting some food together in the kitchen. We gave up on the news, which repeatedly showed scenes of water pouring over the dikes at Lincoln Park and stranded victims being lifted by the National Guard into boats and Humvees.

"Jane?" My mother's voice sounded odd. But I knew this tone; I heard it on the phone when she called with bad news. She beckoned me to the TV. My dad was sitting on the couch, staring.

"And if things couldn't get any worse in Grand Forks, North Dakota . . ." I heard the network reporter's voice before I looked at the TV.

For the downtown buildings to be burning, enormous flames shooting upward, seemed logically impossible. How can fires burn in a flood? In the span of building roofs shown by the wide-angle shot, three or four buildings were on fire, orange flares spurting out windows and pluming from the rooftops.

Cameras panned from high above and then zeroed in on one building, which was being devoured by a gigantic, comprehensive blaze. Gary stood next to me. "Oh my God." The flames seemed to rise out of the water.

North Dakotans are possessive of North Dakota; you have to love it to live there, such a forbidding landscape. Forty below keeps the riffraff out. Laying sandbags, I felt inside and outside at once. These were people's homes, people who were sunk in—generationally and culturally—in ways I wasn't and could understand only as a passerby. I wanted to feel a part, but at the same time I knew I had much less invested in the fight as the town got soaked, its future uncertain.

When the fires began, the story changed. The destructive power of water was slow, gradual, soggy. Fire, though—fire was immediate and complete. Eradicating. Five buildings in our neighborhood were burning, disappearing.

Gary and I had come to love downtown. We learned what to avoid in Grand Forks, the business corridors of Gateway, Columbia, Thirty-second, and Washington streets, where businesses and malls crammed each other shoulder to shoulder. The downtown, even though its quietness was due in part to its decline in business, had hushed, lovely, almost secret qualities. You just had to know where to look. The beautiful red brick buildings of the St. John's block squared off with the Sorlie Bridge. Inside the City Center Mall, a bad idea from the 1970s, when they roofed over an entire city block to form an enclosed mall, there was a funky secondhand shop and a Norwegian dessert shop, and on the upper level, apartments with balconies overlooking the indoor street. The French Connection coffee shop served weak coffee and dry creamer, but I loved it still, its bright colors and palm tree mural, where community theater actors staged a serial drama called Blood Red River, satirizing Grand Forks.

We ate oven-fired pizza and drank Chianti at Lola's, an Italian restaurant, and, occasionally, when we had extra money, we went to Sanders 1907 for pasta. We drank thirty-two-ounce mugs of Killians at the Hub tavern and played blackjack against dealers Gary knew, trying to fill their tip jars. Sometimes we went to Bonzers, a small sandwich shop, for goblets of beer called fishbowls. In the summer I played league softball for Kelly's lounge, a smoky place with boarded windows and electronic dart boards.

The Urban Stampede coffee shop, good coffee with real creamer. Dr. Eliot's Twice Sold Tales bookstore, that smell of books. Griggs's Landing, a blues bar. The Plain Brown Wrapper, a porn shop with a great pinball machine. Murphy's, a rough tavern, no glass bottles allowed and an Elvis lamp behind the bar. The Edge, a nightclub with music pumping its walls. The short walk across the river, either by the walkway on a converted railroad bridge or the sidewalk on the Sorlie Bridge at the town center, took us to East Grand Forks, famous for its Prohibition-era legacy of bars and neon lights. Art deco style and cheap beer at Whitey's, and mounted moose heads, wood grains, and blue nacho chips at the Blue Moose. All of it, open and available, a downtown you could participate in, move around in as you like, everything leveled out, it seemed, by its location way up there, on the way to Canada.

Television report: a fire-bombing plane, the kind used in forest fires, drops red chemical flame retardant on the fires. The plane looks small; the retardant, trivial. These fires could burn the whole place down.

I stayed on the couch and cried into Gary's shoulder, tears soaking into my flood face, making me feel twice as bloated and swollen. I peeked at the screen while Gary watched intently, his jaw slack.

Later I'd be both grateful and regretful we saw the fires through news reports, the story filtered through those lenses, showing spectacular close-ups and overviews of the downtown. We were becoming addicted to the news, which could show us what was happening, sum it up, comment on it.

That Saturday afternoon would become set in my mind with what we saw on television and read in the paper. Camera shots and front page photos. The houses with water to their eaves. The shiny waterfall at Lincoln Park. The Kennedy Bridge, closed, water over the entrance ramps on both sides of the river.

A fireman looking up, squinting, mouth open. His yellow helmet tipped back. Heavy tan coat with a large collar, big camouflage waders to his armpits. His gloved hand rests on the shoulder of another firefighter, with his back to the camera. Above them both, a man in full camouflage stands on the open tailgate of a large truck, water to the top of the wheels. Behind the three men: blue sky, wide column of black smoke, a massive blaze appearing as an orange cross in a partially destroyed building, and the word "heritage" on the corner of an intact white building.

The colors stay with me, that blue sky, the deep oranges and reds of the fires. The camouflage, which seemed strange, warlike. The word "heritage" appearing so prominently, the building sign becoming a sort of promise or a reminder of what is lost.

The newspaper photo captures two disasters at once, the building disintegrating in the background and the immediate plight of the fireman in the foreground. The look on his face records his experience. He can't believe what he's seeing. Perhaps fire was exploding in another building in front of him, or he watched as the planes and helicopters came over to drop their orange chemicals. Looking at the picture makes me wonder what he'll do next. It also makes me wonder about Bill Alkofer of the St. Paul Pioneer Press, who took the photo, and how he traveled the freezing water among the burning buildings of downtown. Like many photos of the flood and fires, it's captivating. It holds a terrible beauty.

When my brother moved to Minnesota, he had long wavy blond hair, the tall lean body of an athlete, and a sort of charm that made everyone—men and women—fall for him. He played bass and sang in a band called Box 10 with guys he'd gone to college with; they drank beer, practiced their songs, and played in bars, traveling back to Iowa, where people knew them, where the evenings worked up into a lather of beer, shouting, and music echoing the favorite bands of Charlie and Kevin, who played lead guitar. Charlie could swing his hair around like Dave Pirner of the band Soul Asylum. When Charlie got married to a girl with long wavy blonde hair and, following her lead, earned a master's degree in education, he moved out to Hastings into a house on a street of family homes across from a golf course.

"I guess you're grown up now," I joked, and though he laughed, he seemed a little uncomfortable in his new skin.

Charlie and I went for walks on the golf course, carrying cans of beer inside our parkas. We lay on our backs in the snow and studied the sky.

"Is this how you thought your life would turn out?" Our conversations always started like that—probing, searching.

One summer weekend Charlie and I arranged to meet in Perham, Minnesota. "That's the town where Vee said they took him," Charlie said. We were in search of the place our grandfather had drowned almost fifty years earlier. Vee—our dad—had never been to central Minnesota, but he knew the names of the towns in the area where his father had died. Little McDonald was the name of the lake, Vee told me over the phone.

Charlie and I went to the library in Perham in search of newspaper articles about the boat accident. The librarian suggested the newspaper office, where we were invited into a back room to flip through large, bound books of single-sheet newspapers from the 1940s. When we found the article, we were stunned to see the words, "Two Drowned; Freak Find of Body is Made" as the headline. We'd been both expecting and not expecting to read the story of our grandfather, who was found by a deputy sheriff named Jahn. He was wading with hip boots, trying to find a wallet lost by Harry Hess, lone survivor of the boat accident, when he spotted a fishing line floating in the water. Thinking a rod and reel might have been on the other end, Jahn pulled in the line. The article, misspelling my grandfather's name, said that the body of H. S. Varly, one of the victims, was on the other end of the line, the hook caught in his trousers.

Charlie and I have this common path in life, it seems—always finding things we anticipate but that turn out to be richer, fuller, more difficult than we could have imagined.

Later, when we asked directions to the lake and walked through a meadow to find it—glistening, clear, smooth to the touch—we stripped off our clothes and went for a swim. The waters were electric on our skin. A fish came near and hovered as if greeting us. We dove beneath the surface, opening eyes to the clean blue waters, thinking of our grandfather, this balance of loss and discovery.

When Gary and I finally cut ourselves off from television reports, the fires seemed to be coming under control. After hours of watching, we imagined a future when the downtown, and possibly the whole town, would be gone, completely gone, as Jen had said. I saw Grand Forks, that city squared off by its containing highways and the river, perfectly flattened into a glittery ash. But the news reports were putting it into perspective, detailing how the chemical and water assaults extinguished the flames.

When we sat down for supper on the back patio, forking various fish steaks off the grill, I was again locked into the combined feelings of excitement and regret. I wanted some kind of definite experience, some resounding conclusion to the last month of sandbagging, the evacuation, Jen's phone call, the news reports, and finally, the fires. I craved an ending or answer. With the fires going out, I knew they hadn't reached our neighborhood, but I couldn't help but think about how they could have burned it all down. What a way to go— sizzled in those fires as the water raged around.

At 9:00 p.m. we headed to the Treasure Island Casino on the Prairie Island Reservation near Red Wing. Come hell or high water, we were going to celebrate my birthday, which Gary kept reminding me with a smile would officially begin at midnight.

I drank red wine, staining my chapped lips. Gary, Charlie, Vee, and I found seats at a three-dollar blackjack table, squeezing in among the other players and people standing around in the crowded casino. Gary and I stayed with three-dollar bets, building up short stacks of white chips on the table in front of us. Vee and Charlie bet red five-dollar chips. It was the best kind of gambling, where we all stayed even or a little above, cheered each other on, chatted with the dealer. Gary asked for mustard seeds and dealer biscuits—the yellow fifty-cent chips he used for tipping.

"Where are you from?" asked the dealer, his hands bending the cards and flipping them into each other as he shuffled between shoes.

"I'm from Hastings. But these guys are from Grand Forks," Charlie said, hitching his thumb at us. The heads at the table turned to look at me and Gary, shoulder to shoulder on our high stools.

"No kidding?" said the man next to me. He wore a Minnesota Twins ball cap and blew the smoke of his cigarette hard out of his mouth, making a white stream. "Did your house burn down?"

"We don't know. We left on Friday and we have no idea what's left." The momentum of the evening was carrying me further and further into the idea that our lives were permanently, irrevocably changed. With all the wine, the noise, the casino lights, and the chips I was stacking and unstacking in front of me on the green felt, it seemed that Grand Forks was, certainly, gone.

"Oh, hey, that's too bad. Get these kids a drink." He motioned to the cocktail server who had appeared again, hovering behind the table crowd. He flipped a five-dollar chip onto her tray.

I reached over to Vee, who was sitting two places away, and turned his wrist toward me to check his watch. It was 11:45. "I'm going to bet my age for my birthday," I said to everyone at the table. "Thirty-two bucks."

"When is your birthday?" asked the guy at the end of the table, playing third base.

"In about fifteen minutes." I moved another three-dollar bet into the circle as the dealer adjusted the cards into the shoe, showed both sides of his hands, and rubbed them together. He smiled at me.

At midnight everyone watched as I counted out red and white chips from my winnings, Vee pitching in from his own stack what I needed to reach thirty-two. I made neat stacks in the betting circle and put two one-dollar chips in the tip circle. "Good luck," said the dealer, knocking twice in front of me on the table. He snapped the cards from the shoe. All eyes were on the card he turned over in front of me. An ace. People clapped and cheered. "Good luck on that ace!" Someone patted me on the back. The dealer placed a card down in front of himself, and then proceeded again from left to right. This time I got a nine. More clapping and cheering. The dealer placed a ten on his down card, a bad sign, since he had been turning over face cards all night, and we all expected him to get twenty again. Vee and Charlie held on eighteen, and Gary held on seventeen. When the dealer finished with the last hand, he put his hands over his own cards, leaned over, and peeked under his ten. He smiled. Turned it over. A nine.

Even while most of the table lost the hand, everyone cheered and complimented my luck as the dealer counted out thirty-two and matched my stack. He pushed the chips toward me.

I got up from the table. The red wine made my lips purple, Gary said, brushing them with his own. We found my mother at a slot machine and played a little while longer, pulling the handle and expecting a shower of gold coins. But I'd used up my luck for the night. I circled an arm through Gary's, and he led me out of the casino, the flashing lights, cigarette smoke, and vague shapes of strangers, all crowding in on me, making me feel warm, strange, and disembodied, distant from my own future.

Union Park

I am ten, maybe eleven years old, hiking the western bluffs of the Mississippi River with my father and big brother, going north toward something my father says is a mystery. We don't know much about nature, not the types of trees or vegetation, and we wouldn't know animal tracks if we tripped across them. We endure the ups and downs of the bluffs as a matter of course, and while we focus on the destination, the hills make a deep, eloquent imprint. They tell the history of water, which cast varied mounds and forged cliffs, gullies, and small midwestern canyons. You can know the shaping power of water without consciously learning it, without discussing it. Our tromping feet teach us shape and form and water.

The woods are dark and safe. When I am with my father and brother, it feels anything could happen, the hills can move or shift or something may be found washed up. We walk what seems like all morning but is probably only an hour, crossing two or three ridges, until we come to what my father promised—patches of broken concrete, chunks of building foundation. Union Park, he tells us, an amusement park with a dance hall, a bowling alley, a pool, a merry-go-round, and a wooden roller coaster. We walk around the ruins, my young mind fixing images, especially the roller coaster. When I kick at a piece of rail embedded in cracked concrete, I see the whole track, even the trolley car, filled with people with big hats and dark clothes.

I know the feel of history before I know actual history. On a summer afternoon in 1919, a heavy rainstorm moved in over Union Park and overflowed a nearby creek. While many people found safety on the surrounding hillsides, a crowd gathered in the picnic pavilion and stood on picnic tables and benches as the park flooded, fed by a foaming, brown wall of water coming from the north. The theater served as a dike, but the flood overtook the main part of the park, where levels rose to ten, fifteen, even twenty feet. The merry-go-round was demolished, buildings collapsed, and the pavilion filled up like a bucket. Reacting within seconds, people outside the pavilion rescued people inside after diving into the rushing creek and pulling them to safety.

The flash flood killed five people. The pavilion, which came to be known as the "Death Pavilion," was never rebuilt, and the trolley cars, once the only way into and out of the park, faded into obscurity. While Union Park reopened after the flood, it never became popular again and finally closed down in 1935.

I take in the mysteries as I poke through the ruins and feel lucky to be a girl in this place, which holds such marvels in the dark bluffs. The park hovers like a ghost in the beautiful hills, and it teaches me to anticipate surprises in the wilderness of woods and rivers.

Six

The Flood

When I turned eight years old in April 1973, it seemed everything happened at once—all in one week, I celebrated my birthday, had my tonsils out, made my first communion, and a tornado hit my hometown, downing part of the Chinese elm in our backyard. Perhaps my mind is confusing matters, combining memories that didn't happen all at once but for some reason center around that time, hard and absolute, like a pit inside a fruit.

Everything seemed so large and beautiful, my life metaphorical in the bigger picture. I returned to the pew after receiving my first communion in St. Anthony's, beneath a ceiling painted with angels, and pressed the wafer with the tip of my tongue. I rolled the fabric of my long dress between my thumb and forefinger, not looking up but thinking of the appearance of the church around me, my grandmother reaching over and laying her hand on mine, catching me in my most private thought.

Twenty-four years later, I woke to my thirty-second birthday adrift on images of the previous day, taken from the screen and matched to my ideas about where we lived, and why. Fire and rising water. It seemed anything could happen. I got dressed and went downstairs to find I was the last one up, and as I poured my coffee, my parents and Gary sang "Happy Birthday." I smiled into my mug.

The morning news showed downtown Grand Forks in ruins, smoke winding upward in thin spirals and the water still running high, creating a flat, shiny surface beneath the charred buildings. The Security Building was gone, only two jagged, burned-out walls remaining. Other buildings remained standing, though their tops had been blasted off. A surprising number of buildings looked stable, intact, until you looked again and saw that a brown river ran through them.

"We're Losing," said the newspaper headline. A fifteen-by-twelve-inch photo covered half the front page, picturing, from above, a wide-angle shot of the downtown area, the symmetrical streets looking wide and reflective. Water. Fire and black smoke shot out of the tops of some of the buildings. The article read like an action story, featuring water so deep the pumper trucks couldn't function, an exploding fire truck creating an oil slick over the water, and a National Guard truck, with a running start, smashing through a fifteen-foot plate glass window to let firefighters into a building through doors held closed by the pressure of floodwater.

In all, eleven buildings had been wrecked by the fires, finally brought under control by an air assault, helicopters and small airplanes dropping buckets of fire retardant and huge amounts of water. Fire trucks couldn't get to the fires— couldn't deliver water because of too much water in the streets—though they finally reached the area on flatbed trucks. The fires died out, their reflections fading into the surface of the river, which seemed to take on new force, new heights, reached by the swallowing of flames.

The flood fight changed. It was no longer about trying to save the town, it was about making sure no one died. Most everyone in Grand Forks and East Grand Forks had left. Thousands of people stayed on cots at the air base, and thousands more found refuge in the small towns of eastern North Dakota and Minnesota lake country. The city's fresh water reserve was expected to run out within the hour. The University of North Dakota canceled classes and called off finals, and President Kendall Baker gave students simple instructions: get home safely.

We clicked off the television and moved to the back patio, where the sun was breaking over the roofs of the neighborhood. I felt tired, thoughts adrift, cut loose from the mooring. I pictured campus, undergraduates packing their bags, some students waterlogged and weary from the flood fight, others care-free, enjoying the upheaval, celebrating their freedom from the toils of final projects and examinations. I imagined them forlorn, defeated in their efforts to help the town beat the flood, or cracking open beers and toasting the river. Which kind of student would I have been?

"I've been thinking about something," I said to my parents and Gary, the thought forming as I spoke it. "All my schoolwork and writing is in the base-ment of Old Science." I could feel my flood face swelling up.

The library and student union had water in them, and the stream on Uni-versity Avenue ran deep. My office in Old Science must have water in it too.

Old Science, which sat on the quad between Merrifield Hall and the library, was a leftover, slated for razing, a catchall for the offices of people and pro-grams crammed into the last available spaces on campus—graduate students, Indian Studies, and the NPR station. With four thirty-foot columns protecting the door, crumbly pale bricks, old smells, and banging pipes, the building felt old school, lovable, if that's where you had to be. I loved the words Science Hall over the front door. I loved my basement office, one big room with desks butted against all four walls, shared with Bill, a gray-haired, big-hearted guy from California, and Yahya, who once asked if I minded if he prayed. "Go for it," I said, as he pointed his rug toward Mecca.

The basement office held many years' worth of my drafts and manuscripts, my ongoing struggle to write poetry, fiction, and essays. I suffered acute writing anxiety, having trouble finishing anything longer than a poem, holding myself to impossible standards, but I always went back to the work, everything assembled in the plastic file boxes I had moved from Idaho to Virginia to North Dakota. I constantly revisited and revised, went back and back over my life and the imagery that seemed to hold answers. I worked at my own past like a miner, someone doing work that had to be done, though I wasn't sure of my motivations, just kept digging away, certain the process was worth the outcome.

My notes for my PhD exams, which I was to take in the coming school year, stayed in the basement office, along with my teaching materials of the last nine years, lined up in a gray filing cabinet. I liked the feeling of accomplishment in academic work, the act of studying, the taking in of words. Reading was like athletics, most of all track and field, when I struggled through the workouts but loved their effects. Interval drills: two-hundred-, three-hundred-, four-hundred-meter runs, then going back down again. Timed rests, the seconds flying by. Oxygen debt. At meets I lined up for the four-hundred-meter hurdles with invigorated fear, and during the race I fought with myself, pushing. Academic work was like that, a mental and physical challenge.

"Grandma's letters are down there." This thought arrowed in. Among all the paperwork I'd meticulously saved were other things—things that meant more to me than anything we kept in our apartment. In her last years, my grandmother wrote to me once or twice a month, and I kept the letters as talismans. My possession of my grandma's letters was my possession of her, of all the women in my family. Along with her letters, I had files full of letters from old friends, connections to my past, all piled up, arranged, and ready for review. I didn't want to forget anything. I never considered what they really meant to me, and now I saw them floating away. Right then, on the patio behind Charlie's house, nothing seemed as important as those papers.

A firefighter. That's what I say I always wanted to be, my alternate reality. My dream job. Even though I know little about it, it's been the job I've imagined for myself if I hadn't taken the path through academics. So what if the papers were gone? Then I could be what I've always wanted to be, reinvent myself. Gary and I together would pursue the unknown, free of the burden of graduate school and living in a town that felt permanent only as long as I was a student. We could go into the western wilds and earn our living with the work of our strong, young hands.

Late morning, Gary watched the news and I stayed at the kitchen table with my mother, drinking coffee and talking about the future. Gary checked in with pieces of news—the water supply running out; the last evacuees leaving by helicopter, boat, and Humvee; and the hospital closing.

My impressions of my life—as a student, teacher, writer, and partner with Gary—crowded in as I sat at the dining room table in my brother's neatly arranged home, his life fixed into patterns in which he seemed, at times, uncomfortable. Like me, he wants to shake out those patterns, trim away the dead or dying branches. Focusing on my life, I was seeing it as a notion, an idea, an act of creativity. What would come next? It was my thirty-second birthday, and I was safe, with my family, while the home we made up north was washed out and destroyed.

I'd never shaken the self-possession of my youth, living in observance of my own life as though it had some broader, significant meaning. At twenty-one, after a summer at home in Iowa, I flew rather than drove back to my college town in Idaho, boarding the plane with a typewriter and a small suitcase. I wore a white V-neck T-shirt tucked into blue jeans. In Boise I took a cab from the airport to downtown, where I had a couple of hours to kill before my bus left for Moscow. I walked up and down the streets looking for someplace to sit down in darkness and write about leaving home and flying into the mountain landscape. I found a sandwich shop and sat at a bright table, too bright for me that day when I wanted darkness, solitude, a completion of the feeling that I had just left home.

Later that day, after snoozing on the bus through the afternoon, I woke as we ascended White Bird Pass. I leaned my forehead into the glass of the window and looked out at the spectacular landscape, with the old highway switchbacking its way up the mountain and giving an expansive view to the distant hills—so large I felt myself shrinking in comparison. From the top you can see the jagged peaks of the Seven Devils wilderness. I was twenty-one years old, and I was coming back to Idaho. Everything I needed I carried with me. I wasn't thinking beyond that afternoon or that view out the bus window. Things at that particular moment were wonderfully, beautifully right.

When I began to take poetry personally—that is, when I saw it as part of my life rather than part of my classroom work—I was astounded by its personal reference. Poetry was a way for me to make a record of those experiences such as the one at White Bird, rising as if I was disappearing into the sky. All those internalized feelings, the ones I kept to myself and that made me feel private, set apart, and a little bit lonely, found their ways out in poetry. The poetry of Idaho, which is so often a poetry of landscape, compelled me. I had moved to exactly the right spot. Poetry was a way of telling and not telling, of expressing myself and yet finding a way to preserve those most secret thoughts of mine, to nourish them. "Everywhere the green trees sway, the grass, the wind, a congregation of solitude," writes Jim Heynen, an Idaho poet. "We will tell no one of this." A centennial anthology of Idaho's poetry, in which I read and reread the section of contemporary poets, included titles that encouraged me to sing of the landscape in ways I wanted to sing, to name the parts: Cabin Note, Out Here, Maybe the Sky, Hometown Bar, Idaho City, Sandpoint, Where You Could Live Forever, One Winter, A Room in Idaho.

My mother and I—my mother is central to my feelings about leaving and coming back to the places I love—sat at my brother's table, speaking softly, reimagining my future. A million unspoken words passed between us, words about how different we are. My mother has spent her life in eastern Iowa, and she is so content there that even a short trip like coming to Hastings for two nights leaves her waiting to get back. The words were also about our similarities, how we look alike, feel alike about so many things, the flowers we plant, the people we meet. She had listened intently to my descriptions of North Dakotans and the Red River valley, forming her impressions along with me. As we talked, we mourned the loss of those things I had come to love, how I had set my roots, like annual flowers, into the northern soil. We pictured the demise of my neighborhood and town, considering Gary's and my future, its erasure, its white space.

When I said goodbye to my parents that weekend of the flood, the fires, and my birthday, I felt as I often had in the driveway in our hometown in Iowa, when I annually left for college seventeen hundred miles away after summers home. It's a bittersweet memory of my coming-of-age years, when I felt so loved yet compelled to disconnect from those who loved me most, setting out into the world on my own, a memory fraught with sweetness and poignancy I recollect as easily as throwing a stone in the water, gentle ripples moving outward.

This time they were the ones leaving. "Please don't go back up there before they tell you it's okay." My mom was still picturing me and Gary returning to Grand Forks in battle clothes, but I had put that idea aside. If we drove back to Grand Forks, we'd have nowhere to go.

We hugged, and I watched as they drove away, turning left out of Charlie's neighborhood, down the street and onto the highway surrounded by corn and soybean fields. They'd take Highway 52 through southeast Minnesota and wind through northeast Iowa to Dubuque, a ride I know well and always feel comforted by, the gentle hold of the river bluffs.

Hackensack, Minnesota. It is one of those typical small midwestern towns, with shops, bank, café, dentist, law office, and churches. But this is Minnesota lake country. At the town's center, a map etched and painted on a large two-legged wooden sign shows all the lakes and snowmobile trails, including the Paul Bunyan trail, a one-hundred-mile, partially paved, reclaimed railway that runs through the city park on its way from Brainerd to Bemidji. Hackensack is the home of Lucette Diana Kensack, the girlfriend of Paul Bunyan, who's from down the road, in Brainerd. The Lucette statue, complete with red blouse and billowing wind-blown skirt, stands twenty feet high on the shore of Birch Lake. Legend says she won Paul's heart when she uprooted two giant pine trees for kindling.

People from all over Minnesota and the Red River valley come to lake country. When they say they are going to "the lake," you don't ask where. Families might visit the same lake or set of lakes for decades, and the specific location is not altogether important, not here in central and northern Minnesota, land of more than ten thousand lakes. Going to "the lake" means, I'm going to relax, nothing can bother me, I'll be on the water, I will be at one with the fish. Maple, Leech, Birch, Elbow, Little Boy, Potato, Washburn, Thunder, Big Rice, Whitefish, Belle Taine, Big Sand, Mantrap, Steamboat, Woman, Pine Mountain. Once you get into lake country, you're at "the lake."

We bought another St. Paul newspaper on Monday morning, the headline: "Hell and High Water." The photo took up half the space of the front page, showing the burned-out shell of the Security Building and a submerged yellow fire truck with a fireman standing atop it, clad in his brown gear and helmet. Water and fire at the same time, a disaster of biblical proportions, ruins reflected in the surrounding floodwaters. The blue sky, the clouds, those firemen perched on the top of the truck, marveling at it all. My head swam.

We headed up the interstate to St. Cloud, where we turned north toward lake country. I read the paper aloud to Gary. The *Grand Forks Herald*, whose offices were lost in the fires, was being printed by the St. Paul paper, tucked inside the *Pioneer Press* like a full-page advertisement. Articles detailed the movement of the flood, telling how on Friday night, standing water leaked out of the north end of Lincoln Park golf course, cascaded into low-lying areas, then moved north along city streets and filled in behind dikes farther north, downstream. Even the EOC, the Emergency Operations Center, had to pack up and move out.

By Saturday morning several feet of water stood downtown and variable amounts spread through the city, and inches—even fractions of an inch—made a difference because the city is so flat. After Friday, when the flood was quick and dramatic—dike busting—it became a disaster in slow motion. Puddles in the streets deepened, became questionable, and then became impassable. By evening on Saturday, 75 percent of the city was underwater, and East Grand Forks was totally under.

The fires began at 4:15 on Saturday afternoon. After a couple of hours of organizing, which included evacuating people in downtown apartments who had ignored evacuation orders, a battalion of firefighters flew over the city in helicopters and forest fire–bombing planes. Over several hours they dumped 120,000 gallons of water and heavy doses of bright red fire retardant. On Sunday morning the downtown still smoldered. Eleven buildings in the most beautiful, historic part of the city had been lost or damaged.

The National Weather Service was still changing its crest predictions, and the river gauge at Grand Forks had been drowned out and ruined. The numbers blurred in my mind as I read the paper to Gary. Friday evening's prediction had been fifty-four feet. Fifty-four feet? That didn't seem possible. During dike-building efforts, the numbers had taken on a palpable reality—we laid sandbags to protect to fifty-two feet, which seemed like more than enough. Now the water was higher—higher than dikes, than NWS predictions, than logical possibility. The times, numbers, and predictions seemed meaningless.

I stopped reading and watched Gary at the truck's wheel. He sipped coffee, his brow furrowing as he contemplated the details from the newspaper. Had the water stopped rising? I imagined the whole region underwater, water reaching as far as the highway we traveled in central Minnesota. A lake expanding to its glacial Ice Age proportions and beyond, taking over the earth.

Pines popped up, closing me in, making me feel near water. Making me feel green. When we arrived in Hackensack, we were buzzed on coffee and news, eager to see our friends and reunite with our dog. Jen and I had chosen Hackensack over the phone, looking at a map and finding what seemed to be the halfway point between her and Brian's campsite near Bemidji and the Twin Cities. Even though we'd never been there, we knew we could find each other in Hackensack, population 245. Gary and I waited a half hour on the open tailgate of the Ranger before the appearance of Jen's red Toyota, arriving from the north.

As we hugged Brian and Jen, the dogs yapped and scratched at the windows from the backseat. They leaped out when the doors opened, and we hugged them too. We all needed a walk.

Brian, Gary, and the dogs headed around the shore of Birch Lake, and Jen and I found a spot on the dock near Lucette Kensack. "Can you believe what happened?" I asked. The last river level we'd heard was fifty-three feet. And rising. On the pier with Jen, I felt buoyed, Brian, Gary, and the dogs in the distance, walking on the beach. Jen took a long drag off her Marlboro.

"We're going back up. Sherry says she has a trailer on her land we can stay in." Sherry was a professor in the English Department and a close friend of Jen and Brian.

"We're thinking of hanging out in Hastings for a while. I don't think we'll be able to go back to the Forks any time soon." I leaned back and turned my face toward the sun.

"You could come up there if you'd like," Jen offered, describing Sherry's farm.

"I think we want to head south again." My head felt heavy. I was hoping for the lake wind to blow through me, lighten me. I had on jeans and one of Charlie's sweatshirts, just right for the fifty-degree weather at lakeside. Even while I tried to abandon myself to the feeling of being outside, soaking in the sunlight, spending time with a friend who was especially uplifting to me, the heaviness returned.

"Do you feel waterlogged? I feel so sluggish and heavy. It's really weird."

"Yeah, I know what you mean. Brian and I have both been feeling like that." Jen paused, took another drag off her smoke. "Do you think your house is okay?"

"I don't know. I keep thinking, so what if it's gone? I have this terrible feeling it's underwater, but another part of me almost wishes it is. You know?"

Jen knew exactly what I meant. We talked about the subversive urge—to wipe it all out, have our lives erased, like a portrait that had been painted, and, not good enough, was painted over.

"It's probably fine, actually. I don't know. I just can't stop thinking about all my papers in my office. They must be long gone by now. I don't know if that's a good thing or bad thing."

My initial mourning period over my papers, feelings I shared so blatantly with my family on Saturday—a kind of Catholic wake for my own recorded past—had disseminated into more practical questions: Had the river washed them away? Were they soaked in their stacks? Unreadable? And if so, what did that mean? Would I throw them in the trash or try to dry them out?

I was glad to be with Jen. We'd had the blizzard together in our apartment, eating scrappy meals and worrying about Miles. Though our campus interests were different—hers in theory and documentary filmmaking, mine in poetry—

I shared the feeling with her of being both inside academics and outside it. "But that's probably how everyone feels," we always said.

"Part of me wants to go back and stay at the base," I told Jen. I wished I could be closer to all that was happening. At the same time I knew I was being ridiculous. Why be up there if I could be comfortable at my brother's house, watching television and taking hot showers?

Jen and I stood, shook ourselves out, and walked as if floating toward the two men and dogs in the distance, walked through time intensified, compacted into the moment. The wind off the lake whipped our hair, and the new spring sun shone through an air so clear it was like an absence of air.

When we met Brian and Gary, we all realized how hungry we were. The idea of food seemed new and so appealing we could hardly wait. At the Up North Café, we sat in a round booth with padded seats and ate comfort food— potatoes, gravy, meat, vegetables. We drank a whole pot of coffee and asked for another. Brian and Jen wondered about their rental house in the country. And Gary's and my apartment—at least it didn't catch on fire, but it must be flooded. It was an old house, and the foundation may have crumbled. What about Josh's apartment? More talking, more coffee.

So what if our homes are gone? Things are always replaceable. Both dogs are outside in our vehicles and we have our health and each other. The river is still rising in Grand Forks, and here we are, 150 miles away, under sunny skies, and we can do anything we like. The Paul Bunyan State Forest is not too far away.

But things aren't right. The coffee feels too hot in my stomach. When I look at Brian, I see signs of my own flood face, that strange swollen look.

The server came back with the check, tearing it off the pad nestled in her broad hand and looking at us over the top of her large plastic-framed glasses. "We're from Grand Forks. Does that make a difference?" I said sheepishly, then felt ashamed.

But it was as if I had said a magic word. Suddenly everyone in the café seemed to be making arrangements for us. They gave us two rolls of paper towels and a huge roll of toilet paper, the industrial kind. They got on the phone to ask about places to stay. They found out the RV park down the highway wasn't open for the season, but it would open for us and we could stay for free. We abandoned our plans to head into the state forest and camp. How could we turn down the offers of these nice people?

Doty's RV Park and Campground, south of Hackensack, was an open field adjacent to a tree-lined creek. The low water exposed narrow, flood-damaged banks, the tall grasses laid flat and littered with debris. Mr. Doty met us on his three-wheeler, saying we should make ourselves at home. There's plenty of space and he'd go on up and open the chemical toilet for us. There was firewood by the barn. Keep the dogs tied up.

"Do you folks have flood insurance?" he asked, speaking loudly over the motor, his hands shaking with the vibration in the handlebar grips. We shook our heads.

"Ya know, it only costs a buck a month most places." He paused, tilted his head, and looked at the ground. "You got yerself quite a mess up there." His hands tightened on the grips, making a slight rev in the engine of the three-wheeler.

"Come on up to the house if ya need anything. We got blankets and winter coats." He wheeled around and was gone.

We pitched our tents and pulled the picnic table into a sunny spot. Even though it felt warm, we knew it would be a cold night, below freezing, and Gary and I had only two thin sleeping bags we took from my brother's garage. "I'm going to go ask for a blanket," I said and headed with Jen across the long camping plain, as open as a football field, and up the slope to the house.

"I wish we'd gone out to the forest," I admitted.

"But then we wouldn't really be refugees. This is kind of fun."

We approached the side door of the house and heard someone rattling around in the garage.

Mrs. Doty was gathering resources, including a stack of blankets and winter gloves. She spoke quickly, directly to us. No introductions. In Minnesota, kindness can be an urgent business.

"Here, take these. You can put the blankets back in here, but keep these gloves. You don't have to give them back." She was busy in her thoughts, imagining what would make us comfortable at our campsite. She didn't ask our names or anything else.

"Do you want a shower? You can take one now. I have plenty of towels. And tell the boys they can come up and take one too." I was surprised by her use of the word "boys."

Jen said she'd love to take a shower, her whole pretty, slender face and big brown eyes expressing her smile. I walked back down to our camp, where Mr. Doty had returned on the three-wheeler. Word had gotten around that we were in town, he said, and the convenience store called. They had a pizza oven and would make us a pizza with anything on it. He held both hands out wide, indicating the size of the pizza. Gary and Brian beamed at the news. "All right," Brian said, his easygoing manner of speaking slowed even further as he savored the idea of the pizza.

Brian followed Jen in the shower and then they drove off to get the pizza. I sat atop the picnic table, taking in the twilight and the appearance of the

Hale-Bopp Comet, which had been visible in the northwest sky all spring, while Gary worked on building a fire, taking particular care with the kindling twigs. Behind us the southeast sky brightened, and when the top of the moon appeared, I remembered the full moon was due. Was the flood still on the rise, pulled upward by the force of the moon? I pictured the Red River valley, an enormous lake suddenly appearing, transposing itself from below onto the face of the earth. As the full moon rose, all that waterscape would shimmer in the light, swelling like an ocean.

Brian and Jen honked the horn and yelled out the window of the Toyota, making the dogs bark. "This is great!" they shouted, pulling in. They had been gone an hour and it was dark. Gary and I sat by the fire, trading shoulder rubs.

"They said we could have any kind of pizza, and we watched them make it." Brian held out the big pizza box. "Feel this thing." We tested its weight. It was heavy, the cardboard moist and hot.

Over the next two hours we savored the pizza, loaded with vegetables including broccoli and red onions, the blazing fire, the dogs asleep at our feet. We talked about what we would do if, back in Grand Forks, we lost it all. We agreed that none of us were attached to the things in our lives, and that we were all, in some ways, rootless, in North Dakota. Our homes were Iowa, Virginia, Connecticut, and Utah, and those were the places where we had deep roots, even if we felt compelled to leave them.

"Rootlessness is an American disease," said David Treuer, a novelist from Minnesota, at the University of North Dakota writers conference that past winter. I had thought it through a hundred times.

"I just can't forgive him for saying that." I was defensive about the idea, feeling accused that by leaving my home, I was doing something wrong. I saw leaving as liberation, as learning.

"I don't think that by leaving somewhere, you really pull up your roots," Jen said. "Can't you come back to your roots?" Moving was a way of gaining knowledge, not an abandonment, we all agreed.

Questions of place were defining for me. Leaving home at nineteen had been invigorating, but returning to Iowa felt like getting back to who I really was. When I began writing during my college years, my memories and imagination often turned back home. Corn and soybean fields, red barns, silos and blue Harvestores, highways that met at right angles, and the narrow forests along rivers and creeks. And the cities, sports tournaments in Des Moines, the oaty aroma of Cedar Rapids, and the location of Davenport, where the Mississippi changed direction and the movement of the sun followed the flow of the water. I couldn't clearly see or completely love my home until I had left it. I needed to think of myself in relation to other places so that I could understand myself in relation to my origins.

At Doty's campground in Minnesota, pondering this sense of place with friends while our current homes were surrounded and infused by the flooding Red River, we seemed to belong no place at all, yet our sensation of belonging in that moment of time was strong. A faint arc of white light in the northern sky is what I saw first. Jen saw it too, and Gary and Brian, who were sitting in camp chairs by the fire, faced away from it. "Hackensack isn't big enough to make that much light. Is there another town up there?" I asked.

"Hey, what is that?" Brian said after turning around in his chair.

The arc quickly became more distinct, and we all stood up.

"Damn," I said. "That's the northern lights."

I had been waiting all my life to see them. The northern lights—the great metaphor of the north. In the same way, I always wanted to see mountains, and I saw them for the first time when I was nineteen, mistaking them for a storm on the horizon at first, and then experiencing the thrill of learning what I was really seeing. In Glacier National Park I pressed my hand flat against a mountainside, amazed I could so easily and distinctly touch a mountain. I first saw the ocean when I was twenty—the expanse appearing just as I thought it would when I came over a rise in the road on the Oregon coast. I walked across the smooth, wet sand, dipped my hand into the frothy surf, and lifted some moisture to my tongue. There was the taste of salt.

We walked toward a field near the campground, all of us tentative and silent, even the dogs. When colors began appearing, we continued north, gravitating toward the lights. The colors came alive, shooting off the arc, greens of all shades and some blues. A swirl of color, low on the left side, contained reds and oranges. Then columns of pure green stretched to the top of the sky, pulsing, like a huge celestial pipe organ. The columns evolved, shifting positions, going through changes so fast the eyesight could barely register them. Ripples moved the whole arc beneath the columns.

Finally, the green columns started pulling back, getting smaller and smaller. The whole scene calmed down to waves, like a light blanket being shaken in wind. The arc started to fade from the edges. I closed my eyes and wondered if when I opened them all the color would be gone, but there remained some green along the top of the arc, and the sky beneath it was pure black. Hours later the sky still held traces of color, though they were difficult to discern and left us wondering if we were the only ones who had seen the fantastic display.

"Oo, ya, anytime they want to put on a show fer us," said Mrs. Doty in the morning when I went to the house to thank her and return the blankets. For her, the northern lights were common.

The Dotys invited us to visit their church basement in Pine River and take anything we'd like from the items they were gathering for a rummage sale. We went shopping—Jen and I modeling shirts and sweaters of all types, Brian and Gary picking through T-shirts. We hugged goodbye in the parking lot, thanked them for delivering Sam. With the appearance of the northern lights, I felt we'd just had a wonderful vacation. I thought of all the light—the full moon, the comet, the aurora borealis—shining down on us.

The northern lights were beyond beauty, like a depiction of life and death, or something in between. When we walked toward the light, we couldn't stop. We could see ourselves as if from above, walking north, in the space between the comet and the full moon that had risen to the very pinnacle of the sky.

Gary said he took his first deep breath in four days, standing in the field, looking at the northern lights. The earth was telling us something with the comet, moon, and lights, there was an incredible story with a beginning, middle, and end.

Though we didn't know it at the time, the Red River had topped out that day at 54.11 feet, almost twice its established flood stage, and held for twenty-four hours. The waters had risen to their full potential, a tide brought to its greatest flow by the power of the moon.

I took Gary's right hand as he drove away from Hackensack, keeping his left hand on the wheel. I massaged it deeply, as he did for me when I drove, moving through the bones, listening for relieving cracks and pops. I felt as though he'd been watching out for me throughout our whole experience of the flood, as if somehow I had become central, my feelings about things we might lose more important than his. Was it because Gary travels the world so lightly, his happiness mobile? He easily moves, picks up and travels, going for a drive on a back road and forgetting everything else. I remembered his backpack sitting on the floor the morning before we were to leave Virginia. "I'm ready," he said, gesturing to the small, battered blue bag, something he took from the lost and found box at the record store after it sat there for a year. Gary was exquisite in his spareness, his lightness.

I loved him from the root. Anything that happened with the flood was all a fascination, a story, not a hardship, as long as I was with Gary.

Lake Itasca

In 1832 the Anishinabe guide Ozawindib led Henry Rowe Schoolcraft to the source of the Mississippi River—a lake, known by generations of Native Americans in northwest Minnesota. Schoolcraft created the name Itasca from Latin words by linking the ending and beginnings of the words veritas caput, *meaning* true head.

Northwest Minnesota, the corner of lake country.

Itasca State Park. Gary and I visit in search of the Mississippi headwaters. We drive straight east from Mahnomen, through the White Earth Reservation, its small towns Roy Lake and Zerkel. At a dusty roadside store, we stop for a pop, savoring the fizz as we drive in, the roads darkened by the gathering trees.

We have come to celebrate my thirty-first birthday, spinning our bikes around the roadway. We find a paved bike path, weaving through the red pine, thinking we would love to jump our bikes off the pavement and onto the pine-needled single-track paths in the forest, but the signs say to keep bikes off. We lean the bikes on a skinny aspen and walk a path into the woods to see the giant Norway pine, 115 inches around, 120 feet tall, and more than three hundred years old.

A birdsong stops us, a spiraling, echoey, descent. A veery, I learn later, when I whistle it for my friend who knows birds.

At the Indian Cemetery we get off the bikes and walk, keeping distance from the burial mounds. I think of bodies squatting beneath us.

At a small side lake, Mary Lake, we lay heads on backpacks and take sun on our faces. It is April, chilly still, the wind cool on our skin. We both drift off until the wind wakes us, and then we peel the plastic wrapping off the pieces of birthday cake we removed from our packs and let warm in the sun. Looking out at the silvery water, we eat the cake piece by piece, melted butterscotch like gold in our mouths.

Riding the bike path back again, we stop on the east side of Lake Itasca, where the wind has picked up strongly. A flock of snow geese spirals on a thermal, like prayers, going northward. The lake ripples and shines beneath them. I want to tell Gary how I feel, but the words catch in my throat.

We have saved the last stop—our visit to the marked headwaters of the Mississippi. We lean the bikes against a fence post and approach. Water spills out of the lake's northwest corner, over a small bridge of rocks, creating a simple, narrow stream, a stream that could carry me home. A tall wooden obelisk stands next to the spillover, carved words reading, "Here 1475 ft above the ocean the mighty Mississippi begins to flow on its winding way 2552 miles to the Gulf of Mexico." Again, I can't speak. Gary is wordless too. We snap a photo of the line of rocks, then step across them, crossing the river. I think of this water as mine.

Leaving Itasca, we drive directly into the sun. We talk about returning in the summer, inviting my brother and his wife to go camping with us. A few months later we'll rent the remote cabin on Lake Ozawindib in the park, swimming, fishing, and resting on the dock of our own private Minnesota lake, and lying in bed at night we'll marvel at the calls of the loons, that sky-sound, a solitary instrument, going on for an hour though we can never get enough, the sound that fills our minds.

The evening of my birthday at Mahnomen, we find a café and eat large helpings of ribs, the meat so tender it slides from the bones. We check into the large casino motel, put on our bathing suits, and slip into the bubbling waters of a hot tub to warm our bodies, which have been chilled by the evening bike ride in the park. We lift ourselves out and return to the room, tiptoeing on the hot skin of our feet, and we make love, our skin flaring at the touch. Later, in the casino, we play video poker, drink salty margaritas, and then head for bed, folding into each other's darkness, the end of a day when it felt we took in a hundred pleasures of the world.

Seven   Dreams

"Concentrate and be patient with the recollection of your dream. Don't censor yourself. The main image from the dream will come forth and reveal itself." Betty held out her palm and moved the other hand along it, as if she were stroking an invisible kitten.

In the sunroom of Betty's house, Gary and I maneuvered old window panes from their casements, soaked them with blue cleaner, and swiped them with paper towels, folding and refolding each sheet. The mother of one of my brother's friends, Betty heard we were staying in town and offered the work. We took the job as much as for something to do as for the extra money while we were evacuated from Grand Forks and staying in Minnesota.

"The dream will tell you what it is about." She carried a perfect calmness. "Simply allow the major image to come forth."

My dreams for the past three weeks had been vivid and recurring. Panoramic views of rushing water and towering fires. I saw them from safe vantage points, on top of or next to the water and fire, feeling their power, marveling at their size. With the destruction of everything around me, I calmly watched from my separate place. Even in dreams, I couldn't believe what I was seeing.

Also, I had smaller dreams, my squeezing into a tight theater mezzanine or walking in the woods in Dubuque, where the trees were dense, constricting. I dreamed of buildings and a bridge with glass sides, of apartments with walls made of stacked boxes. I dreamed my mother drove away in my truck and I lost my vision, and when my sight came back, I walked the streets in New Orleans, trying to find my mother.

We spent three full days at Betty's. When we finished the windows, we went to work in her pasture, pulling out brambles, their weak roots letting go easily but not before their long scrappy bodies tore the skin on our arms. We worked for hours, trying to clear every single bramble from Betty's five acres, a respite of open land behind the strip malls in the Minneapolis suburb of Burnsville. Betty presented us with two crisp hundred-dollar bills, giving us a deep satisfaction with when and how we had earned them.

As a last gesture of kindness, Betty took me aside. "Here, you need this." She handed me a book called *We Sing Our Struggle*, a tribute to Meridel LeSueur, a writer I knew little about. As Gary drove back to my brother's house, I opened the book on my knees and read about a woman with great strength and a deep connection to midwestern landscapes.

In the evenings we loitered at Charlie and Sue's, made pasta meals, and watched videos. We moved fluidly among each other in the kitchen and on the back patio by the grill. We watched movies of all types, checking each other's tastes. I thought my brother might like the films of Orson Welles, whom I'd studied in a graduate seminar—he did, sort of. He thought I might like *From Dusk Till Dawn*—I didn't. He called me a snob, and I called him a lightweight. The table and TV room felt close, familiar, and safe—Sam sleeping at our feet, Lenny the dachshund curling into any available lap, Sue's belly getting bigger by the day, her due date only a month off.

Through news reports and the website for the Grand Forks paper, we checked in on what was happening up north. President Bill Clinton visited Grand Forks to give consolation and hear requests for more federal aid. Gary and I had voted for Clinton and shared a jubilant 1992 election night with friends, ringing out the remote, conservative Republican leadership of our early adult years and ringing in the change. He was good with words, good at giving people comfort. "You have shown that when we think of our duties to each other, our lives are better. No matter what you have lost in this flood, what you have shown the world is infinitely better," he said in Grand Forks. This was exactly the sort of thing North Dakotans would respond to, I thought, as people who could see beyond the immediate problems to the more general meaning. "You give us hope," the Grand Forks mayor, Pat Owens, told him. Standing next to him, she looked the size of a child.

FEMA began setting up trailers in Grand Forks and East Grand Forks. All the schools in both cities closed. The hospital remained closed. No fresh water. No electricity. No food. A few areas on the far west end had remained dry, and people returned or talked about how they never left. Neighborhoods closer to the river remained empty, though residents were admitted for limited blocks of time to assess the damage. Places like Lincoln Park and Riverside, with water to the rooftops, slowly drained, leaving muck-filled, river-stained structures and little canyons under foundations. The reopening of the Kennedy Bridge and I-29 between Fargo and Grand Forks happened quietly, with scattered refugees uncertain about when or how to return.

St. Michael's church, one block away from our house, became our focus as we watched the news. Water had been up the high concrete steps to the church's entry but hadn't reached the church's main floor. In my mind I tried to compare the height of our own front door with St. Michael's, anticipating what we'd find when we returned—a sodden, mucky floor or a dry apartment.

We reached friends through telephone calls and made contact with the university through a phone network. The library, the student union, and other campus buildings had taken on water. I imagined that my office in Old Science, with my papers, was still underwater.

I wrote down everything, keeping a detailed journal, recording the day-to-day events—substitute teaching at the high school, working at Betty's, pruning the lilacs and scattering wildflower seed in Charlie's backyard. Details of our meals. Lessons of domesticity at a time when we wondered about our own home. Perhaps we practiced for what we might need to do or, reaching out far into the future, practiced at a home with some permanency, planting the gardens I often thought about, with their mixes of wildflowers and bright annuals.

My written voice was like a web, other voices moving in and out—how the flood affected the university and city, what my friends said on the phone, Gary's feelings, my feelings. I soaked in news reports like a sponge, taking on their language, their tone. *Grand Forks is devastated. We will rebuild. Citizens have become victims, refugees. What you have shown the world is infinitely better.* I floated through the experience, allowing the major images to come forth.

Though I didn't want to forget a single moment, I struggled with the sound of my journal and the sound of the letter I wrote to my family and friends who wanted to know what was happening, telling them, "We live in the most unique and irreplaceable part of Grand Forks, and knowing our neighborhood is devastated is painful. Most painful, I think, will be returning and beginning to understand the trauma this causes the community."

My own words embarrass me, contradict me, stand outside me. I sound like the people interviewed on TV. Or a politician. Or some public version of myself, a good Jane.

On Thursday, May 8, almost three weeks after we left Grand Forks, we packed up the Ranger with the golf clubs, the cake pan, and our clothes bags stuffed with the donated shirts and pants we had been wearing. We'd leave Sam behind, get him again after we figured out what would happen. Standing in the driveway, hugging goodbye, we felt self-conscious, both serious and so wrought with drama it felt funny.

"We'll call you when we get back." Gary paused. "Oh wait, we don't have a phone."

"Are you sure you don't need anything?" Sue was largely pregnant, a buttoned flannel shirt flapping over her belly.

"Anything you guys need, just let us know." Charlie hugged me to his chest, my head hitting him just below the chin. With his height and thick blond curls, you'd never know we were siblings.

Gary and I took our usual route, looping south of the Twin Cities on Interstate 494 and stopping in the farthest west suburb for coffee before hitting the northwest angle of I-94 toward Fargo. The first time we drove that stretch was 1995. Back then, near Fergus Falls, we stopped at a rest area, alone in the middle of a sunny spring day. A display case outside the restroom held faded newspaper clippings describing an ice-fishing festival and a dog sled competition. I loved that we were moving into new territory, "a winter culture," I said, repeating the phrase I heard on the phone with a UND professor.

But I'd come to know, and dread, that stretch of freeway between Fergus Falls and Fargo. The hill and lake country flattens out to become the Red River valley, and the angle of the freeway creates, I swear, some kind of wind tunnel. In three different winter storms, trying to get back north, I watched cars and trucks careening off the road and prayed I didn't do the same as I chugged along in four-wheel drive. This time the road was clear, though the gray sky seemed close and enveloping.

"Feels good to be driving back, doesn't it?" Gary smiled, took a swig off his water bottle. Being at Charlie's had felt like a vacation at times, but we also knew it had been a long stretch of uncertainty—for all of us—about when we'd leave.

"I can't wait to see what it looks like," I told him. He knew what I meant without elaboration. We were both anticipating the look of Grand Forks.

After we made the northern turn at Fargo, I scanned for water. The ditches north of the city brimmed with water, and the Sheyenne River ran high above its banks and spilled into the fields. Trying to picture Grand Forks, I saw a shallow lake, one we'd drive slowly through like a boat looking for a dock. I saw the entire city afloat. I saw the houses and buildings bobbing in the water. The sun would be out and everything shining.

But there wasn't much water ten miles north of Fargo and beyond. The land along I-29 was black dirt, clumpy in its spring gumbo form, so thick it demands specially designed tractors to pull through it. Halfway to Grand Forks, the American Crystal Sugar factory blew white smoke as usual, rising off the compressed sugar beets. It wouldn't be long before the ridges of beets rose outside the factory, piled high as barns. Everything seemed to be normal. We drove in silence.

Grand Forks, midday. We enter like sleepwalkers, looking for something though we're not sure what. Taking the second Grand Forks exit off I-29, down DeMers Avenue, we are searching, searching, our eyes trying to latch on.

"Is that roof caved in?" Gary points to a building near campus. It looks as if the middle of the roof had fallen.

My breath rises out of the top of my chest. We drive past the building. It's not caved in at all, just an oddly shaped roof, same as it has always been. I have the strangest sensation of dread and anticipation. I'm waiting to see something awful.

Two rumbling Humvees pass, going the opposite way. The curbs wear matted litter. The town feels abandoned, nothing open, no cars in the parking lots of the businesses on DeMers, no lights on in the dim afternoon. Deep ruts mar the shoulders at intersections where Humvees and trucks missed the pavement under the floodwater. We take a left on Washington and pass the white water tower, the goofy one painted with a winking smiley face. This is nothing like I imagined it would be—this street we saw over and over again on the news, the water knee-deep. Now it's dry, a dusting of dirt covering everything.

"Are you glad to be home?" I ask. Gary nods, slow motion, as if his head is underwater.

Where the hell is the water? We don't see any, not even a puddle. Everything looks dry, dirty, and cold. The sky is gray.

All the buildings, all the houses look as they did before. Or do they? We drive on, no problem, as if nothing had happened, no water, no barricades, no collapsing buildings. We turn, as usual, at the Knights of Columbus. But that building looks odd, too dark. Are the windows gone? One block more and we get to our house. It is standing. Did I expect to see it like this?

We park out back, and I step lightly through the yard, looking for evidence. We'd heard about contamination, all the sewage and oil and who knows what else that had soaked into the lawns. I look at the house, the crumbling spot beneath the furnace vent on the back wall. It looks bad, but it has always looked that bad, right?

We walk together purposefully, up the steps, through the front porch, and I watch Gary turn the key in the lock. He swings the door open. The apartment is dim, and though I can't see much inside, I focus on the carpet, the beige, furry surface where I've wiped up a million muddy and snowy footprints. It's perfectly clean. It's dry.

We hugged in the doorway. "It's dry!" we both said. I felt like someone was watching. Was I on TV? A flood victim, returning home to assess the ruins? I acted, but didn't feel, happy. A major northern river had flowed through our yard, through this building. I felt, along with other things, a serious amount of regret. I felt disembodied. We went inside to find the refrigerator door standing open, revealing an empty, clean refrigerator.

"Hello?" Our neighbor Marielle clumped down the stairs. She'd cleaned out the fridge for us after returning the day before. It was a bad scene when she arrived, she said, both our apartments reeking of rotten food and leaking juices from the depowered refrigerators.

"Marlene let me in." Marielle wore a vibrant pink tank top and multicolored skirt, looking, as she so often did, too tropical for the cool temperature.

"So, you had to leave?" I asked.

"*Everyone* had to leave," she said but didn't offer details. Marielle was always a little annoyed with us, always short on words. I usually felt the same, but this time I was glad to see her. We found out later from Tracy, a mutual friend, that on the Saturday morning of the flood's crest, Marielle stood on the porch upstairs, waving a pink scarf. The National Guard loaded her and her cat, Cleo, into a boat and drove them to dry land.

We thanked Marielle for cleaning out the refrigerator, a kindness that had taken us by surprise. "Not a problem." She paused. "Robert and Marlene haven't been over yet to take care of Josh's place. I don't know what they're going to do about it." She turned back toward the stairs and her regular seclusion in the upstairs apartment.

An incredible smell drifted up from Josh's apartment downstairs. With a flashlight we descended the dark, misshapen stairs, stopping when we could get a view into the main room of the Cave. Black, smelly mud covered every-thing, and the contents of the apartment were scrambled, as if the place had been picked up and shaken. A stained afghan lay on an overturned chair at the center of the room.

"Wow," Gary said, reaching a hand out to the wall to steady himself on the slippery stairs. I looked in over his shoulder.

"I wonder if he's seen it," I said, thinking about Josh. I was fairly sure he hadn't been back. I'd spoken to him the previous week on the telephone in Montana, where he was staying with his family.

Even with all that we'd moved up to our apartment, Josh's apartment looked full, everything flushed out of the corners. We tiptoed back up the stairs, Gary with his hands on my hips to guide me and steady himself.

I wanted to go to campus immediately. It was as though I'd been writing a script, foretelling the ending. I couldn't resist the power of the story, the rising water, the workers on the dike, the evacuation, water filling the town, the buildings disappearing beneath ragged flames, and now Josh's apartment in ruins. What would happen next? The falling action, the denouement?

Later I'd think about how in my secret, half-formed thoughts I was already imagining new frontiers, Gary and I trudging away with our few belongings, leaving behind all that was waterlogged or burned. The load would be light, the memory heavy. Our lives would change completely.

We drove up University Avenue, past the stadium, the student union, the library. Everything looked the same, but dark—lights out in the gathering dusk. We took the one-way street that cross-cuts campus to the parking lot near Merrifield Hall. Old Science sat at the center of the rectangular campus, which is contained east by the interstate, north by Highway 2, west by Columbia Avenue, and south by railroad tracks. So much of Grand Forks seemed squared off. Squares inside of squares. And beyond those squares, filled in by the campus and the town, were empty spaces. Out on the prairie the squares opened up into vast, seemingly endless dimensions.

The squares of campus, almost two miles from the river, had been filled by water. It was hard to see how the river could have come this far, until I remembered the description of the flood as a lake. *Ten miles wide.* The river had swallowed the English Coulee, the campus waterway, making it part of the same flow.

Yellow caution tape strung on rods encircled Old Science, the word "danger" in black. My key no longer worked in the front door. We rounded the building to the window wells above my office, and I got down on my knees, knowing what I'd see: it would be dark, furniture tumbled around, like what we saw in Josh's apartment. Gary handed me a flashlight and I shone it in the window.

Blue carpet. My chair pushed in. The papers on the desk, stacked as usual. The cheap, plastic bookshelves, with my carefully selected and arranged collection, just as before. The gray metal file cabinet, my anchor, secure.

The air went out of me. I looked up at Gary, and we said the same thing. "It's dry."

I had the strangest feeling. After three weeks of waiting, all I needed to see was a mucky mess, to turn away from it, and be relieved of my work. I wanted out, but I didn't want to quit. It wasn't clear at the time, but perhaps I wanted something larger than me to answer my questions and take on responsibility for my future. I wanted a future driven by something better, my own willfulness replaced by a greater force.

I had already determined my own loss and begun mourning it. How could I turn those feelings back now? Three weeks earlier I sat on the back porch at my brother's place and cried for my lost papers and for the uncertain future. The tears kept coming. My mother looked at me, her eyes just like mine.

Did I lose anything? Now that we were back in Grand Forks, it seemed we had lost nothing at all.

When I moved to the white North, I clutched my doubts as if they were full satchels, pressing them to my chest. Reading, writing, hashing out ideas had been pleasures for me but also raised questions. Was this the kind of work I wanted to devote myself to? Where did I belong? I liked the idea of disappearing into the whiteness of the North, walking away into a kind of bliss, the sky enveloping me. Now that I'd seen the sky, living with my gaze turned upward, what came next?

Some of my friends understand when I say I wanted to see all the work saturated beyond rescue. To be swept away in a flood as though God had come down and made a change. Nature would change my life.

Ron McFarland, my MA adviser at the University of Idaho, wrote me, "If it were my writing, I'd be glad. Then I'd start all over again, and this time, do it right."

There was something so appealing about the prospect of losing that work and my years of writing, my self-definitions, that when Gary and I walked toward the window, the solid ground of spring beneath our feet, I felt charged with anticipation. When I shone the flashlight into the window, I wanted to see blackness, the realization of loss. I wanted a halting conclusion to hit me where it counts. One definition of myself, as a writer and student of poetry, involved a desire to be ripped away, submerged. So much for those papers I hauled with me on my wanderings around the West, to Virginia, and now to North Dakota. Where better to lose them than the big, bold landscape of the prairie with its endless sky?

I looked into the basement and saw my life had not changed. I would remain as myself, as I'd always been.

Midwest Floods

My parents live on Grove Terrace in Dubuque, Iowa, in a blue house tucked in the side of a bluff, in a neighborhood of angled streets. When they talked about buying the house in the spring of 1992, they said they "bought a view, with a house attached." The deck is enormous, like a wooden platform set up to view downtown Dubuque, the Mississippi, and the opposing bluffs of Wisconsin and Illinois.

It had been raining for weeks when I went to see them in the summer of 1993, and rivers all over the Midwest ran high. Nothing could soak into the saturated ground, and even the air felt like water.

During a break in the rain, I rode my bike to the lock and dam, where we used to hang out as teenagers. The paved road runs atop the permanent flood wall, a long slope of riprap, where we sat on summer nights drinking Dubuque Star beer and Boone's Farm wine, procured from trips over the toll bridge to Wisconsin, where the legal age was eighteen. We smacked our shins on the various sized boulders as we crawled up and down.

I pedaled past cars and trucks lining the loop at the marina and the road up to the dam. People were out looking at the flooded river, which was closed to boat traffic. Debris clogged the gated entrance of the lock and tossed in the churning water beneath the dam.

A man with sun-wrinkled skin watched the water's rough surface. A fisherman, probably. A woman, impatient with the unlikely traffic jam, poked her head out her window and beat her fist against the side of her car. Two couples walked one behind the other, holding hands, laughing. Another biker nodded to me as he raced by, outfitted in tight biking clothes. The line of traffic advanced slowly toward the turnaround at the dam.

My parents were annoyed because they couldn't play golf. They were mad at the sky and the way it kept dumping gray rain, over and over, causing humidity headaches. We sat in the house, remembering how lovely it was to be under the blue sky, nothing but breeze and birds and a long fairway.

But these feelings, born of frustration, didn't go very deep. We spent the mornings looking at the *Des Moines Register*, reading stories of the floods.

Water in central Iowa spilled over sandbags or levees to wipe out homes, city streets, and corn and beans in the fields. In the black and white newsprint, the water looked dark gray, sometimes black, filling in places it shouldn't be and causing people to stand rigid, as if they were filled with the sand they had just shoveled into bags.

When I was growing up, midwestern rivers had always been a comfort. We used to swim in the Mississippi, and after the shock of the initial plunge, the water became soothing. Even though I am not much of a swimmer, the river put me at ease, its current insistent but embracing, and I could let myself go. The 1993 floods wrecked farms and overtook towns, wiping people out. The rivers had seemed to take on a different personality. In Dubuque all remained dry because of the five-mile flood wall built following the big flood in the year of my birth.

I went for a drive north of Dubuque on the Great River Road. The atmosphere darkened, black clouds spreading to fill the whole sky as I wheeled my truck up the curving highway toward the small town of North Buena Vista. My best friend Jenny and I used to drive this highway on hot summer afternoons, looking for adventure in Buenie, as she liked to call it, where we'd roll into town as though we knew everyone, and look for beer and boat rides.

At the marina the river ran so swift, dark, and high that I felt I could see its cross-section. The water seemed to be levitating above natural levels. Boats bumped against the aluminum roofs of their slots at the marina, and people idled everywhere, standing in the streets and slowly driving by, waiting to see what would happen next.

When the rain began again, I drove into the Turkey River valley to get on Highway 52. I wanted to leave the river road, get away from the water. The rain kept coming, adding to fields that had become ponds. Ducks swam in the pastures. Farther north, above Guttenberg, I drove up the hill that gives a view over the town and the river, and I saw what the national news had been showing, how the islands were underwater and cabins looked as if they were floating in the river's center.

The current flowed above any prediction, any interpretation. When I returned to my work, my new marriage, and my usual life out east, how could I describe this, how everything seemed changed? How everything seemed flooded, even the air. As I watched the river come up against the flood wall in Dubuque, my parents reminded me about the last time this happened, in 1965, during the week of my birth. I live in the memory, as if I was created by flooding water.

St. Mary's bell tolled sonorously, and on the deck on Grove Terrace, I felt the sound throughout my entire body. Then the rain began abruptly, and the sirens in East Dubuque, where the river was rising into the city streets, started, whirring furiously as the storm's wind whipped the branches of my parents' linden tree. The two sounds came together in the wet sky over Dubuque, and it seemed the deep pitch of the church bell tried to calm the rush of the high siren.

The massive flooding of 1993 affected Iowa, Minnesota, North Dakota, South Dakota, Nebraska, Kansas, Missouri, Illinois, and Wisconsin. On the Federal Emergency Management Agency's list of top ten natural disasters, the 1993 flooding ranks fifth and the Red River valley flooding of 1997 ranks ninth in the cost of relief, $1.141 billion and $740.1 million, respectively. Water, dollars, levees, diversions, maps, mitigation, insurance, warnings, and recovery.

The 1993 waters forged a new definition of the Midwest, vulnerable flatlands where most of the natural wetlands are plowed under and where the runoff of precipitation tests the capacities of rivers and streams. When they fail the test, we're left wondering how and why. We build the dikes higher, but the water still comes, threatening and enlivening us. Floods change the way we see everything.

Eight

Returns

We were all moving things inland, but there was a gigantic, unstoppable flood on the way. They started moving cemeteries, pulling the graves up on shore.

Journal entry, mid-March

Everyone in North Dakota talked about water. In Grand Forks the spring flood was an annual worry. In central North Dakota the Garrison Dam creates one of the largest reservoirs in the United States, Lake Sakakawea, the waters of the Missouri River held back in 178 miles of pooling blue waters one-third the length of the state. In east-central North Dakota there's an infamous water problem at Devils Lake, which the Army Corps of Engineers has been working on for years. The lake has been rising since 1940, and in 1993 it rose five feet in six months. More than eighty-one thousand acres of adjacent land were flooded, and the city of Devils Lake is constantly threatened by water. When the lake was at its highest level, estimated to be eight hundred to twelve hundred years ago, it spilled into the Red River valley. Now, on a rising trend, it sometimes overflows to Stump Lake. In the 1990s the lake rose more than twenty feet, and the surrounding residents had to transplant houses, roads, and neighborhoods.

Grand Forks was fortified by the permanent dike system to fifty-two feet, which seemed like more than enough space for the flood to drain through the tunnel between Grand Forks and East Grand Forks each spring. But in 1997 the flood was far larger, far more unpredictable than anyone had imagined. First, they called it the flood of the century. Later, with theories about the history of the floodplain, they called it a five-hundred-year flood. Fifty-four feet every five hundred years? Numbers took on the resonance of the Bible, Noah and his three hundred cubits by fifty cubits by thirty cubits. Forty days and forty nights.

For the first month after the crest, people returned one by one and family by family to see what happened. Some people were homeless and had to move into sudden, stark trailer courts made up of dun-colored, rectangular, windowless FEMA trailers. In flood-damaged houses, getting utilities back on was a step-by-step process involving evaluation by electricians, replacement of breaker panels and fuses, inspections to meet standards set by the city's Mechanical Board, appointments to energize meters, FEMA inspections and paperwork, and purchases of new water heaters and furnaces. Scheduling appointments and finding the hardware to get power back were daunting; the city had too few inspectors and electricians, too little equipment, and sky-high fees. I heard on the radio that we should be suspicious of con games such as the door-to-door sale of grossly overpriced electrical panels, and uncertified electricians and repairmen looking to take advantage of flood victims.

Our landlords had pumped out the basement but hadn't been back to the house. Ours was only one on a long list of their emergencies. We used extra blankets, bottled water, and a portable propane camping stove. "I like camping, Beej," I told my mother on the phone, "but not in my own apartment." I ran a hand through my unwashed short hair, stiff and cold.

Gary went back to work right away, the motel filling with journalists and emergency workers from FEMA, the Small Business Administration, and North Central Electric. Downtown the remains of the Security Building, built in the 1870s, had been razed, leaving a mound of ash and bricks.

The tops of other buildings wore ragged black crowns. Windows along the streets were shattered or boarded over. Broken glass and other debris layered the sidewalks and curbs. I looked in windows. In Popplers Music a piano was thrown against the stained and cracked storefront window, its keys coated with mud drying into curls. Metal shelving lay on its side, matted sheet music spilling out. Black cases crammed the edges of the room. Music washed away in the flood.

Our favorite hangout, Whitey's, was totaled. We'd logged hours in the smoky booths, carrying in our logo-enhanced pint glasses—"Have a Primo night!"—on Thursday nights for the Grain Belt Premium special. Whitey's had vintage menus with photographs of pork chops, steaks, and mashed potatoes; pastel lights that illuminated our faces; and a stainless steel horseshoe bar. We walked across the foot bridge, a converted railroad bridge, in all weather to gather in the booths with our friends and work on the world's problems.

The steel around the base of the bar still gleamed, but everything else inside Whitey's was darkened and destroyed. Knee-high debris covered the floor, booths, chairs, and tables, jumbled and broken to pieces. In the Side Bar the fish tank remained in its place on top of the bar, but the fish were gone, freed in the Red River.

An intense smell wafted up from the sewers all over Grand Forks and East Grand Forks. It occupied the cities—a gray smell. Dirty. It overwhelmed my senses, getting in my eyes, in my nose, my mouth. I thought my skin began to smell of the flood.

The persistent gray of the between-season, North Dakota's postwinter but not-yet-spring, dominated the skies. All the dirty mounds of snow had washed away, but a feeling of winter remnants still hung in the air. It was chilly, only forty or fifty degrees in the daytime. Using a port-a-john on a street corner while our bathroom was out of order, I had to stand up and brace myself against the sides so that it wouldn't tip in the buffeting wind.

Robert, Marlene's husband, came to inspect the house. He disappeared into the basement and came back with clenched teeth. I asked if everything was okay.

"Okay? What do you mean?"

I was unsure how to ask if we'd be able to stay. "Is the foundation all right? Is it okay to live here?"

The look on Robert's face suggested I had just asked the stupidest question in the world. Then his face softened. "It's fine. You don't need to worry about it." I didn't want to ask about anything else, though I was concerned by what was beneath us, all the murky wreckage. I'd been hearing horror stories of crumbling foundations and contamination. Some houses in our neighborhood, while they looked fine on the outside, had massive, hidden damage. Gary and I had navigated the mess in the basement to get a look at the walls, running our hands across the bumps and cracks in the old foundation.

Robert was unconcerned. "This place is fine. You should see some of the others I'm dealing with." He managed other houses in town and had his own home to fix up, where water had damaged the first floor.

The local AM radio station was in emergency mode, broadcasting information and taking calls. The whole town seemed to be standing on weak, saturated legs or ready to collapse into sinkholes. The people who called in sounded distraught. "There is standing water in my basement. What am I going to do? I don't even want to touch the stuff." There were instructions on how to get through things one day to the next, pumping out water with portable generators, keeping the house livable without heat or water, salvaging waterlogged furnishings. Stores reopened and immediately sold out of essentials: bottled water, rubber boots and gloves, buckets and mops. Gary and I, hungry for something good to eat, went to the west side of town to one of the few reopened restaurants. We devoured scrawny chicken breasts wedged into hot dog buns, served up on a paper plate. At least the food was hot.

The weather just wouldn't come around. By the end of May daytime highs were still only in the fifties. We had no electricity, heat, or gas for the stove, but the tap water came back, so cold it made our hands burn. Something needed to be done about the basement, where Josh's things lay in ruins and the smell persisted. He hadn't returned from Montana and called to say he wouldn't be back anytime soon.

Our landlords agreed to pay us an hourly wage to clean up and tear out the basement apartment. With supplies left at our front door by the Salvation Army—buckets, mops, bleach, and brushes—we set to work. Tentative at first, we tiptoed around the tumbled furniture, the kitchen cabinets dislodged from the walls, and the misshapen refrigerator, remembering our cozy home. I tried to see it with Josh's eyes, with all his things warped and ruined and covered with a slippery mud containing oil, sewer waste, and river silt. Everything had to go, down to the studs behind the walls. Like almost everyone else in town, we made a refuse pile at the street curb.

I picked up two saucepans, one in each hand. "These look fine. Should we save them?" I said through the surgical mask I wore to prevent breathing in toxins.

"I don't know. The thought kind of kills the appetite, doesn't it?" Gary picked up a coffee mug missing its handle.

We lined things up in the backyard for a hosing-off process.

"Are these papers a total loss, or should we try to save them?"

Gary shook his head. "This stuff is all contaminated. I don't think it's worth it."

There was no sun and the wind picked up. Not able to simply pitch the notebooks and folders of paper onto the junk pile at the curb, I laid them in the grass and tried peeling apart pages, though they were glommed together in flood mud. I took a hose to Josh's books, shooting fresh water down the spines and into the pages until my hands were freezing. When I squeezed the books, brown water came out. I stood them on their spines and opened the pages toward the breeze.

Half the yard was covered with Josh's papers and books. When they dried, the wind lifted them, flapping pages and matting single sheets against the neighbor's fence. Eventually, I gave up, placing the papers in clumpy layers on shelves in the garage. I couldn't bring myself to throw them away.

In recent weeks we had reconnected with people, assessing losses. We'd spent an afternoon with a writing professor with whom I'd had a difficult relationship, our ideas about the teaching of writing different and contradictory. Kathy's house sat behind a steep dike at Riverside, and it had been totaled. "Want to see the house of horrors?" she asked when Gary and I arrived with others to help with the wreckage. Kathy showed us kitchen cabinets that had curled out from the bottom like a girl's hair, a butcher knife that had lodged in an electrical outlet, and a ski boot in the toilet. Kathy's eyes shined, her mouth tightening at the edges, indicating stress. Mostly, however, Kathy revealed a mystified amazement at losing everything, and she showed unwavering determination. "They may just plow the whole place under, but let's get this beast out into the yard," she said, laughing, as four of us wedged her swamped refrigerator out the back door. Kathy's and my disagreements about editing and composition theory seemed distant and petty.

Gary and I also paid a visit to the home of Jay and Martha Meek. Jay was my mentor and dissertation director, and we'd worked carefully on poems, one word at a time, in his book-lined office in Merrifield Hall. He had a Campbell's soup can pencil holder and a big window facing the quad, which Jay gazed out, hands clasped behind his back, like a ship's captain. He was private, reserved, brilliant. When Jay and Martha returned from their spring sabbatical, they found a home that had been filled with water to the second floor. Gary and I went to their home by invitation to help with small chores after they and their daughter Anna had dealt with most of the mess on their own. They provided a picnic in the yard and adopted out to us a beloved houseplant, a prickly pear named Old Possum, otherwise known as Blue Boy. They kept their losses close, as they kept so much of themselves, with a dignified silence.

The Coast Guard came to North Dakota to help. In an interview, one member said it was out of his experience to be in a place so far from water. Far from water? What was he talking about?

The water receded quickly, and though it still ran against the dikes, it was far beneath its crest level of fifty-four feet. Most of the town was dry, except for the lower lying neighborhoods where houses were submerged.

I heard something creepy. I heard that in the medical school on campus, in a basement, cadavers were floating.

A group of people with white and red Salvation Army T-shirts pulled over their sweatshirts came over after they finished a morning's work at the house across the street. Three big men went together into the basement while I chatted with the others outside. They had taken a bus overnight from Minneapolis and would be in town to help for the day. "There's nowhere to stay," said a woman who protected her clothes from flood mud by wearing an upside-down garbage bag, holes cut out for her head and arms. The men in the basement emerged up the narrow concrete stairwell with Josh's refrigerator, heaving it onto the junk pile. Then the entire group vanished as quickly as it had come.

I learned how to use a crowbar and tear walls from their studs. Gary threw a sledgehammer into the thin particle board wall at the back of the apartment, the one we had so carefully reconstructed after Sam, in a fit of cabin fever, tore it down two years before. Gary had labored at fitting a new cheap door, which replaced the old cheap door Sam wrecked, onto the doorframe, finally giving up and getting our skillful neighbor to do it. We inspected the surface of the wall, where we had so diligently worked with a can of spray-on surface texture to match the original. Gary, laughing, heaved the sledge into the wall.

All over Grand Forks curbs were piled high, some as high as six or eight feet, forming tunnels of junk on roadways. Homes were cleared of their mud-damaged furniture, carpet, walls, clothing, books, toys, blankets, kitchenware, photo albums, and artwork. In the rush to clean up, people debated what was salvageable and what was not. You weren't allowed, by a mayoral injunction, to salvage anything from a pile that wasn't yours, a ridiculous idea to some. My friend Elizabeth, who had lost two thousand books in her basement, said she found a perfectly good ceramic mug in her neighbor's pile.

"You didn't take it, did you?" I asked.

"Of course I did," she replied, frowning at me and then laughing.

Pulling an old paint can and a warped piece of wood from the wreckage, I painted a sign: "D'ya like what we've done with the place?" The next day, long after spring should have begun, I woke to see the pile and sign dusted with snow.

Of all the inconveniences, it was the lack of hot food that got to me most. When I heard the beeping of the Red Cross truck, I went outside, taking whatever meal they were serving. Gary and I picked through the foam containers with their various incarnations of hot meals. One time I bit into something unidentifiable.

"Is this meat or cheese?" I asked Gary. He didn't know.

I wrote another letter to friends and family, this one handwritten on yellow paper. "Our neighborhood is ruined. And everything—air, grass, and sidewalks—is so badly contaminated that you can practically feel the effects in your body."

Our neighbors Dee and Mark worked ferociously at the garden in the warm months and at snow removal in winter. One of their daughters was the picture of a rebellious teenager, complete with low-slung jeans and cigarettes. Their eight-year-old was a pigtailed blonde who followed her parents around like a faithful dog. They had come back a few days before we did, pumped out their basement, and begun dealing with the thick coating of mud, working day and night on their home.

I listened to Dee, who leaned over the picket fence and smoked, the two of us like a tableau of neighborly, chatty women (never mind that the picket fence was corroded with flood mud or that we were wearing knee-high rubber boots). Dee said she couldn't return to her restaurant job until they got the house in order.

"We've got to make this place livable before I can do anything. If they want to fire me, let them fire me," Dee said.

"What are you working on today?"

"Well, we've got the water heater guy coming today, and that's the last of the big stuff. Once we get that pile off the curb, I'll feel a lot better." She dropped her cigarette, crushed it out, picked up the butt.

"Looks like you've got a nice pile going too." Dee gestured toward our sludge pile on the berm, which was reaching new heights now that we were taking out walls.

As we dismantled the Cave, I listened to call-in radio shows about the cleanup. I heard long exchanges on methods of cleaning and preservation, such as how to boil and bleach a child's toy or how to safely remove a flooded-out furnace. You couldn't hire anyone to fix your problems, because every business in town was dealing with its own flood damages. "Don't go down in that basement," my mother had warned me over the phone.

"There are eighty-five-year-old women mucking out their basements, Beej. There's no one else here to do the work."

Doing the work felt good. As we closed in on finishing the basement, I felt a sense of accomplishment. I wanted to clear the whole space and wipe it clean, make it new.

The people playing blackjack at the Ramada were driving Gary crazy. One group, working for the Small Business Administration, was from Texas. They showed up as soon as Gary opened his table at 5:00 p.m. and described their work on flood relief, heroic by their standards. Their pride in being Texan constantly leaked into the conversation as they drained big mugs of Budweiser. "Real high rollers," Gary called them, as they played the five-dollar maximum, complained about bad cards, and swept back their winnings as if they were cleaning out a Vegas casino. Gary worked alone, without breaks, his dealers still gone.

I started going to the Ramada in the evenings rather than staying home in the dark apartment. The lounge felt safe and warm, illuminated by the light of the big screen TV. Our friends joined me—Melanie, Simon, Rex, and one or both Steves—and we poured glasses of light beer out of a pitcher and ate popcorn. The lack of hot food at home made me greedy for the popcorn, its grease, its saltiness. I couldn't get enough.

Rex had lost everything. He ignored the evacuation orders in his downtown apartment, cozying in with books. Stocked with supplies, he wanted to experience the flood and stayed in the way that I had wanted to, digging in, watching the water. He'd lost his sense of smell in an accident the year before, and while many downtown residents ran from their apartments at the smell of smoke, Rex continued napping, undisturbed. He woke to a pounding on his door and firefighters commanding him to leave. Immediately. Rex grabbed his backpack and left everything behind, exiting his building to see enormous flames shooting from windows. A precocious undergraduate English major and established voice in the community as a writer for the *High Plains Reader* alternative paper, Rex lost every word he'd ever written to the blaze.

Our experiences seemed a strange mix of dread, loss, and preservation. Steve, a transplant from England who held a PhD from Rutgers and served as director of UND's writing program, could put things in perspective with a fascinating articulation born of his love of Samuel Beckett and the contemporary British dramatist Dennis Potter. It wasn't until months later that I fully understood what he'd been through during the evacuation. He; his wife, Donna; and their eight-month-old baby, who was running a high fever, caught a crowded Northwest flight to Donna's hometown in New Jersey, sitting in the only available space, the crew seats. Steve returned on his own a couple of weeks later to help with cleanup and prepare a summer class.

The conversation never ran dry. We talked about sandbagging, the weekend of the fires, what we did while we were gone, how it felt to come back. We couldn't stop talking about what had happened, but later, when I try to recall these conversations, I can't remember the particulars. The stories that seemed so rich and symbolic eventually deflated, the details lost like receding waters. What are the enduring images?

When I first returned to Grand Forks, standing in line in a gas station convenience store, one of the few places open, I heard a man say there were houses "still floating" on Lincoln Drive. I drove to the neighborhood and found it closed off with plastic traffic barricades, then went home, pulled on winter gloves and my long biking pants, got on my mountain bike, and pedaled back, past the road blocks, to the top of the short hill leading down to the houses. The water stood at first-floor window level. The man's comment made me think I was going to see houses adrift, bobbing in the water. These houses looked grounded, but they had shifted, had been jolted from their neat lineup in the street. It was like seeing a terrible injury, bones protruding from beneath the skin at odd angles. The water around their foundations stood still, not the strong north-flowing current I expected.

I tipped the bike onto its side in the drying mud and walked on the dike, recalling the night Gary and I were there. Were we risking our lives? Sandbags remained in loose, skewed stacks on top; others had tumbled, like dead soldiers, down the slope. Remnants of white plastic from the bags were caught in treetops. Down in the flooded neighborhood, the water looked black and still.

An RV had crashed through the side of a house. A trumpet dangled from a tree. A picnic table stood upright on a roof, as if ready for a tablecloth and picnickers. A station wagon sat on top of a collapsed garage. Porches were pulled away from houses, leaving gaps between the landing and front door. Some of the houses looked undisturbed, as though families could still live there, though the darkness emanating from their windows suggested the opposite. A subtle pall covered it all, gray and brown. A film of the river. The smell was powerful, an old rotting smell, everything saturated and unable to dry out.

Painted words appeared on the houses: "Go away." "Take your pictures elsewhere." "Home sweet home." "Wipe feet before entering." "I said a Bud, not a flood." "Fifty feet, my ass."

Later in the summer many people would roam this neighborhood or sit like sentries in the front yards, fending off looters (forty below doesn't keep out all the riffraff). I tried to imagine looking down on a home I owned, seeing my neighborhood ruined. The mad shift of perception when something so familiar is damaged, taken away.

When Josh came back, his boyish face looked different, puffy. A young-looking twenty-four-year-old with his thick brown hair, he seemed even younger now, maybe a teenager. The sun had finally come out, and we walked back to the garage in short sleeves.

"I tried to clean these off, Josh."

Josh picked through the papers on the shelves for a few minutes, lifting with the tip of his index finger a muddy mass, peeking between layers. The outer layers of mud had dried, but inside it remained wet and smelly.

I saw him look at a pile of letters, pink envelopes. He looked away.

His golf clubs soaked in a tub of water and bleach. He picked one up, stepped out of the garage, and took a swing. The club made a tinkling sound, like something had broken loose inside.

"These might be okay," he said, holding the club in both hands out in front of him, like he was presenting it to me.

"How about this?" I had scrubbed off the leather and plastic folder that contained his high school diploma. The paper of the diploma, behind the plastic, was wrinkled and stained.

"Yeah. I might take that."

A stack of notebooks slumped against the side of the garage.

"Do you want to see those?"

He moved his hand toward them, waving them off. "We can get rid of them." He again looked at the club in his hands, as if he had never seen a golf club before and was trying to figure out what it was.

"All that stuff can be trashed. I might take the clubs, though."

Josh and I walked back toward the house. "Where are you going now?"

"Back to Lynn's." He had been staying with his girlfriend.

Josh and I hugged in the backyard, and then he was gone in his little blue car. I stood in the garage and looked at the papers, thinking of my own papers, how I had felt their loss. And then not lost them. The basement in Old Science had something called a subbasement, I'd been told. By the time the subbasement filled, the flood had begun to recede from the campus, and Old Science lucked out, no water in the basement offices. "Stayed dry so they can raze it properly," joked my friend Bill, who, along with me, was angry about the plan to do away with Old Science. Soon I'd be packing those papers up again, all dry and neatly arranged, and moving them somewhere else, though they seemed heavier now, harder to take along.

I pushed the toe of my shoe against Josh's notebooks, nudging them apart, and then I pulled on rubber gloves and got to work, throwing it all away.

I take a long walk because I can't warm up. Even my bones feel cold. I loop around the north edge of town, near the cemetery. Puddles fill low spots among the graves, and my shoes get soaked in the saturated ground. I see a low place, a puddle in the distance, and I don't know if I'm seeing it right. Are those caskets, half-submerged in a pond? Why would they be left like that, unearthed? Who's in charge here? I hesitate to go closer, thinking of the bodies adrift, moved from their resting places, but I can't stop looking at them, and I return the next two days, keeping my distance but trying to understand what I'm seeing. On the third day they're gone.

When the landscape was transformed, our consciousness of how we construct our lives changed. I don't know if I actually saw the container of a body lifted from below, but my mind holds this image as central to the experience, when the community I was coming to know was shifted, raised, submerged, and revealed in ways no one could have predicted.

I'd carefully arranged my life, kept records of who I was, where I was. When I imagined the ideas washed away, I felt a lightening, an invigoration. I'd be free of myself, start over, go back to white space and begin again. It wasn't because I didn't like the person I had become—more the potential of discovery, the chance to see everything new. I craved new experience, new landscapes. I could begin again, with real work, see the results, firm and absolute, in my hands.

I hadn't considered fully enough what it meant to stay, to negotiate, like the old river of my hometown that had been so long on its path, though it was always changing in ways I didn't recognize.

Devils Lake

I have been lucky in love, sharing with my husband a desire to move, change, and explore. My own movements come from restlessness and a greed for landscapes—I can never see or know enough. His movements are less willful, expressing his malleability, an openness to change such as I've never known in another person. We rise and go together.

Saturday morning, late summer in North Dakota, after we've come through our first year. We study the map, searching for another place to explore. We've been to Kelly's Slough, Turtle River State Park, and Agassiz National Wildlife Refuge, where we learned the wilderness of space. Today we intend to head farther out, and we drive west on the straight shot of Highway 2.

"I'm loving this drive. I don't care if it takes all day to get to the lake," Gary says as he cranks the window handle.

The atlas sits open on the seat between us, showing the blue spot of Devils Lake cozied next to the Spirit Lake Reservation. Promising symbols, tiny outlines of tents and pine trees, indicate state parks and recreation areas around the lake. The fluid, resonant music of the Cocteau Twins blares from the cassette player, and Gary and I ride with windows down, smiling, hair flying. Our camping gear is packed neatly into the back of the truck, and Sam snuggles in between two sleeping bags, sleeping soundly under the safety of the topper.

In western Grand Forks County, the trees thicken, rows and rows of protective shelterbelts planted along the edges of fields, so thick in places that they look like small forests. Gary's coworker told him the county had the "most shelterbelts per square mile in the country," and we'd laughed about that, wondering who kept track of such things.

We pass through the extreme flatness of the Red River valley into a more diverse landscape, more arid, with gentle rises. We don't know it, but we're driving up and out of the Red River valley, its sandy edges indiscernible to us, newcomers. Farms give way to wide open fields, and the sky, when seen in relation to the variable shapes in the land, becomes extraordinarily huge.

Signs of civilization fall away, and the few towns off the sides of the highway seem quiet and hunched beneath the dominant sky.

Yellow-headed blackbirds appear, lighting on the tips of swaying cattails. A shadow of hills rises on the southern horizon. We pull off onto a gravel road and get out to check the wind, which has been rocking the truck. It is ocean wind.

Prairie. Farms and towns don't change the essential quality of what we see and feel, the openness and gorgeous simplicity, land and sky.

Approaching Devils Lake, we turn at the first brown sign, a recreation area called Shelver's Grove. "Closed" notices are posted over the camping signs, and at the picnic area, water laps up like a lazy tide, drowning the swing sets and picnic tables.

"This is creepy," Gary says, pointing to the foamy surf.

"Hey, no skeeters." I unbutton the flannel shirt I had pulled on in anticipation of North Dakota's relentless mosquitoes.

"Let's check out another part of the lake."

We pass the city of Devils Lake and turn south, where we find a stretch of road that looks as if it floats on a flat plain of water. Rock embankments seem to hold the road up. "It feels like we're driving on top of the lake, doesn't it?" Gary observes. People fish off the sides of the road; gulls wheel around in fast, wind-whipped circles.

By late afternoon we give up on our ideas about beaches and settle on Graham's Island park, on the far west side of Devils Lake. We ignore the eerie flood scene, again with submerged playgrounds and picnic tables, and find a grassy hillside campground. Empty. The lake is strange, we agree. The flooded shoreline parks look long abandoned. But when we park the truck, set the dog free, pitch the tent, and get busy at making a fire, we no longer worry about the water. Twilight hangs in the air for hours.

With my favorite Swiss army knife, I slice a green pepper, mushrooms, a yellow onion, and potato chunks, folding them with butter and garlic into foil packets.

"Well, it isn't what I expected, that's for sure." I poke the fire.

"It's nice in its own way though, isn't it?" Gary stands behind me, pressing his fingers into my shoulders, knowing how to squeeze the thoughts out of my mind.

Later we walk to a meadow above our campsite. The full moon, whose rising we missed behind the woods surrounding the lake, had climbed into the sky and lit the meadow in a white glow.

We are silent, grateful for the surprise moon. "Is that the brightest moon we've ever seen?" We savor our luck as we have so many times before, when something in nature appears, half familiar, but looking so incredibly beautiful we can hardly believe it. Rhododendrons under snow on the War Spur Trail in Virginia. The shape of a wolf in clouds over Superior National Forest in Minnesota. The incredible green of the Salmon River in Idaho, where I took Gary on our honeymoon.

Though it seemed strange and a little frightening, the lake was near, beckoning, fascinating. The waters were rising, had been rising, with a mind and momentum all their own, for years.

Nine

Recovery

I will listen to what you say.
You and I can turn and look
at the silent river and wait. We know
the current is there, hidden; and there
are comings and goings from miles away
that hold the stillness exactly before us.
What the river says, that is what I say.
                    "Ask Me," William Stafford

Water has been my freedom and my solace, my teacher and my guide. As long as I can remember, I've been pulled toward water, my internal divining sharpened by my home geography, where the river, even when not in view, was strongly present. I always knew north, south, east, and west by the river, by understanding where I stood in relation to it. In my girlhood I learned to love my home—especially the Mississippi River of my hometown, which seemed as vast as an ocean because of its unknown reaches north and south, yet steady and dependable, shimmering in sunlight or freezing into icy sheets where we dared to walk on water.

Even the few family stories that have come down to me seem focused on water. My maternal grandfather, a giant of a man with legendary strength, caught a thirty-pound, forty-two-inch catfish in the Mississippi, and when, as a girl, I studied the newspaper photo, I understood the magnitude—the fish had been hauled out of the mysterious depths of the river. My grandfather seemed capable of such miracles, a man who commanded water; he swam, he once told me, from Iowa over to Illinois and back.

My father's father was long gone by the time I entered the world, taken away by waters. Only when my brother Charlie and I went to Perham that summer day in Minnesota could we understand the few details our dad, Vee, had told us and more fully imagine what happened during our grandfather's fishing trip in 1946. Harold, known as Sam, and three others were overcome by a squall on Little McDonald, a lake near Perham. This grandfather, too, had strength and agility, a lean, scrappy man who was a war veteran and semiprofessional basketball player. The boat tipped, and he and his friends clung to it, but Sam had a shoulder injury that prevented him from keeping his grip in the raging winds. One man survived to tell the story. The next day, when the deputy sheriff searched the lake, he found a snagged fishing line, followed it hand over hand, and discovered in the tangle my grandfather's body.

My mother's fear of water infused my sense of self and of the world around me. Secretly, I rebelled against her fear. Her attitude created a boldness in me—my desire to lay claim to that which she dreaded and denied. As I began to follow my waters, coming into womanhood, I did so in a private, independent way so that my mother wouldn't worry, so that my grandfathers' legacies would be observed, and so that I could find my own way across landscapes, propelled by the force of water.

The facts rolled in: more than 11,000 homes and businesses, of an approximate total of 15,000, were damaged in Grand Forks. East Grand Forks was completely underwater, with only 7 of 5,500 homes remaining dry. Seventy-five percent of Grand Forks's fifty-two thousand residents and 90 percent of East Grand Forks's eighty-seven hundred residents were evacuated. An estimated $1.5 billion in damages was reported. At the University of North Dakota, 72 of the 238 buildings on campus were damaged, and the total cost in damages and recovery reached $43 million.

The Red River crested at 54.11 feet, more than 26 feet above flood stage. The last crest prediction by the National Weather Service had been 54 feet. While many people blamed the NWS for missing the mark, the service said the flood showed how predictions are affected by a variety of unpredictable factors—the variable rate of the spring melt, the freak April blizzard, the constricting dikes up and down the valley, the swirling waters on the abnormally high water table. The peak flow in the city limits was 137,000 cubic feet—more than one million gallons—per second. Bill Clinton visited the cities, followed by Elizabeth Dole and Newt Gingrich. FEMA gave household reimbursements, business loans, and temporary housing. Corporations, such as AT&T and Pillsbury, gave money and supplies. Tom Lehman, the professional golfer, gave $100,000. There were pledge drives, donations, and matching funds. An anonymous donor, who turned out to be Joan Kroc of the McDonalds corporation, gave $2,000 each to flooded-out households, for a total gift of $20 million. Then another anonymous donor gave several more million dollars. Thousands of people arrived by plane, bus, and car in Grand Forks and East Grand Forks to volunteer for cleanup.

Checks and boxes of supplies arrived from Gary's and my family and friends—our parents, aunts and uncles, cousins, old friends, a Catholic high school in Cedar Rapids, Iowa (whose principal was a friend of my family), Gary's family's church in Roanoke, Virginia, and my niece, who organized a bake sale at her school.

We felt like the whole world was watching. And sending support. I learned a sort of gratitude that comes—and there's no other way to say it—with an overflowing heart and that changed the way I think. *I feel the light air of my life,* writes Jay Meek in a poem.

By midsummer, with buyouts of destroyed homes underway, structures were coming down. I rode my bike in the dusty streets but stayed clear of the low-lying neighborhoods where people's homes were backhoed and bulldozed into piles of debris. Other homes, damaged beyond repair or implicated in the temporary blueprints for the new dike system, remained like specters on streets where the destruction was less visible and conclusive, awaiting their fates.

The mounds of debris on berms began to disappear, changing neighborhood streets from junk tunnels to nearly normal. The city landfill loaded up, with estimates for refuse amounts as high as a hundred thousand tons. Gary and I watched as yellow machines cleaned up warped and sodden mounds on both sides of our street. A large backhoe took a long time with a washing machine, nudging it against a curb and then lifting it into a dump truck.

Jim McKenzie told me the North Dakota Museum of Art was training volunteers for an oral history project, collecting flood stories. "I think you'd be really good at it," Jim said. I appreciated his faith in me, much as I appreciated my recruitment by another professor who asked me to help at Sandbag Central during the flood fight. Most of all, I didn't want to miss anything, drawn to the imagery and stories of the flood, addicted to the narrative.

Fifteen people chomped on doughnuts and sipped coffee on a Saturday in the museum's basement. I knew some of them. Jim was there, along with a few instructors from the English Department. A historian from the Baylor University Institute for Oral History held us in rapt attention, the room silent as she put into general terms the thoughts and feelings of our fragmented conversations about the recovery, the mucking out, the assessment.

"Disasters accelerate both personal and community changes or trends that were already in motion," she said. "There is survivor and rescuer guilt, a feeling that we should have done more to help others, and that, compared to others, we had it too easy." She talked about the determination to rebuild in people who lost their homes and the vague emotional experience of those who had not lost so much.

Outside help is appreciated, she explained, but sometimes donations can be inappropriate or miscalculated, castoffs from other people's lives. I thought of our pepperoni, how for weeks we'd been eating cold, thin slices, peeling them off the two large rolls given at the curbside outside the Salvation Army center at the mall.

She also explained that after a disaster, people suffer a loss of innocence. People in Grand Forks might feel they had trusted the environment, felt secure in it, and that a disaster can shatter faith and show we can't control everything. Still, people will rely on quick redemptions, explaining the flood to themselves: North Dakotans are resilient. We will rebuild, we will come back stronger. The flood brought us together as a community. Perhaps it was meant to be.

She raised questions about the word disaster. How real was this disaster? No one died.

Oh yes, people have died, insisted some gathered at the table in the museum's basement. There had been at least one suicide in Grand Forks since the flood, and many elderly people, dislodged from their permanent homes, were dying. In this state with its big sky, airy atmosphere, the fluidity, the comings and goings of weather, the people and towns grew deep, and some could not survive the tearing out of roots.

"Our society doesn't acknowledge place attachment," said the historian. "How do you grieve the loss of place?" But in North Dakota, a place where you know every day where you are living, where people speak often and expansively of the land, the valley, the Europeans and Native Americans who came before them, I thought some grieving was happening, conscious and direct. Madelyn Camrud, a local poet, told me how she walked into the backyard at her condemned home and shouted at the river, "How could you do this?" She said she couldn't look at the river for weeks but eventually found that her respect for the river had deepened and that she better understood the spirit of water. One of her poems describes how on the day she moved out of her home—soon to be demolished with a backhoe—she thanked God for the river.

So much of the conversation at the museum was about loss and reclamation. Grand Forks and its surroundings had been reclaimed by the past, glacial Lake Agassiz, which returned and materialized, ghostly in how quickly it came and left again. Because my connection to the community felt tentative, based on my time there as a student, I felt I hadn't lost much at all. Still, I had my own questions of place attachment. Was the flood helping me know this place better or preventing me from knowing it, spurring on the feeling that I should leave and find new territory? I had wanted to retreat into white spaces on the map, and the flood both created that disappearance and made the place more vivid.

My friend Steve spoke about how we tried to make the flood meaningful, how we needed to talk to make sense. I thought of the bowls of popcorn we had eaten at the Ramada and how we could talk for hours, going back over the story, searching for details, combining the meanings that might somehow allow the whole thing to make sense.

For me, the story needed some kind of ending. The historian's ideas brought some of my thoughts into focus. While much of the town labored at recovery, I was adrift, the bottom of our house cleaned out and our apartment safe and dry—though still cold and dark. Our apartment held the many comings and goings of students, only temporary in Grand Forks. As much as I had come to like the town, even to love our neighborhood, I didn't think of it as permanent, as a place where I would stay.

I had some sort of need for disaster, for loss, along with the rest of a town where people lost everything. I needed the physical evidence of loss so that I could really feel what loss was about, wanted to be affected by fate—even if the terms were awful brown waters.

When the surroundings change, the people within them change. Lake Agassiz had risen again, come to take the place of a landscape that had seemed certain and reliable. Even with the waters dried up, I knew—we all knew—we lived in a place of water. We had come to understand it deeper and better.

The stories at the museum shared an exigency, and I recognized how the flood made me turn inward, trying to make sense, trying to tell the truth. But truth is relative, and the stories, too, contain the silence of loss. Some people left Grand Forks, and others chose to stay and get to work, without so much introspection and analysis, without so much talk. The stories reveal who we are, full of words, ready to say what happened to us, as well as silent, turning back to the cold muck of a basement, reaching in and ordering a new kind of life.

In July I rolled over in bed and reached down on the floor for my T-shirt and shorts. It was great sleeping weather, fifty-five degrees at night and perfectly clear. The mornings were crisp and clean with air it felt good to breathe, and daytime temperatures reached the seventies.

I began the daily ritual of getting coffee supplies from the kitchen and starting up the Mr. Coffee balancing on a windowsill. An extension cord connected the coffee maker to the neighbors' fully powered house.

I heard something new in the kitchen—the distinctive buzz of electric power—and I swung open the door of the empty refrigerator to a beautiful sight: the interior light came on. I reached over to the light switch on the wall and flipped it up, looked into the glare. "The lights are on!" I said, rounding the corner into the bedroom, where Gary was half-awake. He left the bed, arranging his crooked boxers, and gazed into the overhead light.

Electricity in the kitchen was a portent of better things: two weeks later the gas came back on, which meant hot food and water. I resumed my evening soak in the claw-footed bathtub, where I read books and studied, dripping on my notebooks.

A few weeks later the electricity was restored in other rooms in the apartment, and just before winter threatened, the new furnace was installed. "I never thought I'd want to celebrate having lights in our apartment," Gary said, smiling widely as he flicked a switch up and down, making flashes in the living room.

I drove to Hastings to see the baby, Jack, who had arrived at the end of May, and to pick up Sam. Sam barreled through the foyer toward the door with his watchdog bark, saw who it was, and gave me one of his rare smiles, lips pulled back to bare all his teeth.

Charlie and Sue were amazingly relaxed with the new baby, who fit remarkably into the flow of their life. Charlie played with Jack's wet hair, puffing it up in front and combing it back. "Sort of looks like Christopher Walken with that hair, doesn't he?" he said, turning the portable baby swing around so that I could see.

The University of North Dakota opened its fall semester as usual, with only a 4 percent drop in enrollment, less of a decrease than had been expected. Gary worked all the time, it seemed. Even with my flood brain—a condition many of us suffered, a lack of concentration—I finished up two projects from my spring graduate seminar, one on Keats's ode to autumn and one on William Carlos Williams's "The Desert Music." I taught classes and began preparing for my doctoral comprehensive exams, making a study plan, beginning with primary works of the writers I needed to know for the four areas I was being tested on.

Studies settled on me like a thick blanket. The flood was with me at every moment—some days at my particle board desk, I heard trucks working downtown, beeping as they backed up, clearing the rubble of burned and flooded buildings. I wanted to help in the recovery process, but I didn't know what to do beyond going forward with what I was doing in Grand Forks in the first place. When winter came in, cold, snowy, and intense, it seemed grayer than in years past, the sky sinking closer to the wrecked, jumbled community.

I closed in on the PhD examinations, studying in the library during the day, and during evenings, at our kitchen table, I alternated working a jigsaw puzzle of sunflowers in a field and reviewing stacks of note cards. There was no need to read anything new; all I had to do was remember.

Gary and I prepared to celebrate our fifth wedding anniversary with a trip to Biloxi, Mississippi. The trip had been planned for more than a year, since my mother asked if we would like to join her and my father for a golf and gambling vacation. For a few hundred dollars apiece, we bought a vacation package including several nights in a motel and a few rounds of golf. We could gamble all night long in the Biloxi casinos.

Gary and I, accustomed to mountain bike outings and hiking rather than resort vacations, decided we'd like to do something different for our anniversary, and the trip with my parents seemed right. With all expenses added up, our savings account, a recent venture, almost exactly covered the costs, and we took it as a sign that we should go.

The wide beach at Biloxi was gray in February, the sand cold and hard under my bare feet after I was determined to get a feel for the place with my shoes off. The sand had been transported in, we learned, when Biloxi was made into a resort area. Mississippi mud spread across the beach, swallowing up the sand particles with its sticky grayness.

While I know the basic geography—that the mouth of the Mississippi is only thirty miles to the west, near New Orleans—I didn't anticipate that the waters of the Gulf of Mexico at Biloxi would be so riverlike. I walked out into the shallows, and the feel of the water against my shins and knees was familiar. I could close my eyes and be home again.

Consciousness of my upcoming exams wove its way into my days, at the front of my mind during the quiet, focused activity of golf, and moving to the back when we entered the louder escapes of our trip—a Mardi Gras parade in Pass Christian and our evening trips to the casinos. Gary and I stayed late at Treasure Bay Casino, playing video blackjack for twenty-five cents a hand and listening to the same cover band play the same songs every night. My parents went to bed early and got up for their morning ritual, the breakfast buffet and slot machines.

I had my stacks of note cards and stole a few hours for memorizing. I asked Gary to help, and one afternoon we went to a restaurant with a wide-open view to the gulf. He sat across from me, note cards in front of him like a deck of cards waiting to be dealt.

We progressed through, the names of novels, poems, short stories, and critical theses coming easily to me, trained into my mind in long rows of details. I liked having this knowledge; I felt as though I'd filled in the gaps of things I wanted to know, things I hadn't had time for. The experience of studying at the kitchen table in our small, spare apartment, way up north, was crystallized into the literature, history, and philosophy written on the cards, which I could recollect with one-word clues.

Out the window the Gulf of Mexico shined, a completely flat, waveless plain. My mind opened to the details of my studies, everything laid out level and revealed. I felt the beauty of knowing, the beauty of seeing. I'd come such a long way, through so much land and water.

I expected an ocean, but the gulf had turned out to be different, the cross-tides of the big southern waters meeting my home waters, the Mississippi, all those miles from the obelisk at the top, where they say it takes a drop of water ninety days to make the complete journey.

Here was a place where I could see and feel the meeting of waters, an answer to the unknown reaches I used to imagine when I was a girl. Here was an answer, a conclusion, an ending. And like any good ending, it seemed the start of even more.

We are more water—I am more water—than I have understood, not the observer of landscape as much as a part of it. When the water recedes again, we are left alone with ourselves, part river now. I was rising, like the current that surged and captured its surroundings.

We can't control everything. Nothing is permanent. In some ways I'd already lived my life by acknowledging this, keeping moving, resisting permanence in where I chose to live and how I lived there. Perhaps I had been living that way, however, with the belief that somewhere there is permanence waiting for me, that someday my choices will become absolute and defining. Perhaps I'd been living in fear of something that doesn't really exist. Permanence is no more real than the look of the water in the fields, transforming Grand Forks into a waterscape that had come and gone as quickly as a change in seasons.

The flood created sensory memories for me, when every moment felt alive, every nerve end in me dilated as I took in the beauty of experience. My memories became my secret. My friend Elizabeth, an accomplished English professor, who in the midst of the flood marched up her street in boots, carrying her friend's dog in a carrier, and volunteered herself to the newspaper after its offices burned down, told me, "I was so happy during the flood." I didn't ask for elaboration. I knew exactly what she meant.

What is my most valued possession? The intangibles. My freedom, my marriage, my family. I value my own body, my physical health. What about all those papers in the basement of Old Science? They were a metonymy, I think, something standing for the whole. I dreaded the importance they had taken on for me. I couldn't get rid of them, but I wanted them gone.

The flood wiped them out after all, making them seem no more than a fact, just papers to be stacked neatly on my shelves or just as easily thrown in a sodden pile on a city berm, loaded up, moved to the landfill. How easily they might be washed away. When the papers are gone, what happens to memory? I wonder at how we live our lives through our records of it, as experience comes and goes, moving in and out on the tide of memory. The present holds as much or as little meaning as we devote to finding it.

Grand Forks and East Grand Forks have been forced to deal with wrenching questions that few cities ever face, questions about flood forecasting, home buyouts, business development, and a water protection plan. The cities would change shape. Who could and couldn't keep their homes? How much were the houses worth? Who belonged where they started, and if they had to move, where were they supposed to go? Hundreds of homes were already ruined or had to be destroyed. Businesses moved; roadways closed down; schools and churches reorganized; and new neighborhoods rose up, with some potential buyers skeptical of the costs and appearance.

Every spring the communities watch the rising waters with trepidation and, I think, a deep knowledge of the river. East Grand Forks constructed an "invisible flood wall" by the spring following the flood, a low wall with grooves to add partitions as needed when water rises. Grand Forks relies on temporary levees of fifty-two to fifty-four feet. For the long term, a project led by both cities and the Corps of Engineers begun in the summer of 2000 involves a combination of levees, flood walls, diversions to coulees, and a wide greenway. The projected completion is in 2006, and the improvements will cost three hundred million to four hundred million dollars.

Downtown Grand Forks has a Flood Memorial Park where the Security Building used to stand. The roof on the City Center Mall was removed, and several buildings were torn down or renovated. There's a new corporate center and county office building. East Grand Forks constructed a new business area called the Riverwalk. The Whitey's original building had to be demolished, but the owners preserved the stainless steel horseshoe bar and rebuilt a block farther from the river. The Blue Moose made a spectacular move, the intact massive log building hoisted onto a flatbed and moved fifty yards across the street, onto higher ground. East Grand Forks also has a new library and City Hall. The Red River State Recreation Area, replacing destroyed neighborhoods in the floodplain, has opened in the heart of the town, so when we visit, Gary and I can camp across the river from where we used to live.

It's the first nice day of the new spring season, April 1998. We take a drive to Kelly's Slough, the wildlife refuge west of town, a place defined by what happens in the sky—migrating birds come and go with the seasons, and planes take off and land on runways on both sides of us, the airport and the Grand

Forks Air Force Base. Three ponds frame an open view to the surrounding landscape, which is incredibly flat. Though the floodwaters didn't reach this far west, they could have if Lake Agassiz had returned in full form.

The sun is high in the clear blue sky, and we've taken the back way. On the gravel road we roll down the windows and shiver in the not-quite-warm air. We park and let the dog out the back. Everything remains snow and ice covered, that layer of winter firmly set over this vast terrain, but we see signs of spring, like small patches of open water in the wetlands.

The projected crest for the Red River flood this year is around forty feet. The ice and snow in town are almost gone. There is nothing to worry about.

We feel triumphant. We've come through another North Dakota winter, getting out for cross-country skiing and ice skating, but, mostly, quietly living inside. We watch the sky for new birds to appear, though we're a little early for the spring migration.

I've learned new ways of seeing. Everything seems to exist in relation to where we stand on the observation deck. The close range holds splatters of bird droppings and carved initials on the wood of the deck. The far range holds tree lines, buildings, and a water tower.

I can picture North Dakota from above, close my eyes and see Grand Forks, crammed into a square acreage on the sea of prairie, with that meandering dark line of the river going away to the north and to the south. I've come to love the containment of the image. And I think of the people too—tough minded, thick skinned, defined by their attachment to a stark, difficult landscape.

I wanted to find a remote, distant border, but I discovered that North Dakota is more a center than an edge. It contains the geographical center of North America, a stone cairn marking the spot. Canada rises above the straight, steady border, its tall provinces breaking out into the ice and waterlands of the far north. Though I expected to be getting away when I moved to North Dakota, I felt I was living somewhere much closer to the middle.

It's a beautiful day and I want it to last a long time. I want to stay here with Gary and name all that we see close and far: patterns in the white splatters; carved letters, numbers, and hearts; an unidentifiable bird high above; a jet above the airport; a jet leaving the air base; goose boxes; shelterbelts; scattered houses and farm buildings; the smear of a cloud; each other; the sun.

My need for new landscapes has transformed into capaciousness. My whole sense of who and where I am has risen and expanded, has taken on cycles, like the North Dakota seasons, of becoming first empty and then full. Now I feel ready to focus on what is in front of me—while keeping my maps always in reach.